THE THREE Cs:
Children, Computers, and Communication

THE THREE Cs:
Children, Computers, and Communication

TOM STONIER
School of Science and Society,
University of Bradford
and
CATHY CONLIN
Head Teacher,
Norton Glebe Primary School,
Norton on Tees, Stockton

JOHN WILEY & SONS
Chichester · New York · Brisbane · Toronto · Singapore

Library of Congress Cataloging-in-Publication Data:

Stonier, Tom.
  The three Cs.

  Includes index.
  1. Computer-assisted instruction.
  2. Computer-assisted instruction – Forecasting.
  I. Conlin, Cathy. II. Title. III. Title: 3 Cs.
  LB1028.5.S813 1985   371.3'9445   85-16937
  ISBN 0 471 90828 2 (pbk.)

British Library Cataloguing in Publication Data:

Stonier, Tom
  The three Cs: children, computers and communication.
  1. Computer-assisted instruction   2. Microcomputers
  I. Title   II. Conlin, Cathy
  370'.28'5404   LB1028.5

ISBN 0 471 90828 2

Printed and bound in Great Britain by
Biddles Ltd, Guildford and King's Lynn

To the children of the world —
may they communicate in peace

Contents

Acknowledgements

The authors are most grateful to Marlene Ellison for her invaluable and dedicated help in the preparation of this manuscript.

We would also like to thank the staff and students at the School of Science and Society of the University of Bradford, and the staff and children of Norton Glebe Primary School for their co-operation. We are particularly thankful to Ken Price of Phototronics for capturing on film the children's various and sundry computer activities.

Lastly we acknowledge with gratitude the permission given by MVDP to reproduce the MAKATON symbols on page 121.

The opinions expressed in this book are the authors' and do not represent the official views of any of the various institutions and organizations with which the authors are affiliated.

Prologue

Sometime,
during the second half of the 20th century,
   Western Society evolved from an industrial
      to a post-industrial, or to be precise,
an Information Society.

Education for an industrial society
         centred on teaching the *Three Rs*:
'Reading, 'Riting, and 'Rithmetic'.
Its aim was to produce
   a disciplined workforce −
      punctual, conformist, specialized −
         to operate
the brute machinery of the nation-state.

Education for an information society
         will centre on the *Three Cs*:
'Children, Computers, and Communication'.
Its aim will be to produce
   a creative workforce −
      adaptable, entrepreneurial, interdisciplinary −
         to help solve
the problems of this planet.

Section I
Computer-based education

Chapter 1

Introduction

The first genuine revolution in over a century is beginning to over-take the education system. This revolution is based on the emergence of cheap home computers and will bring about a shift from school-based back to home-based education.

Such a forecast is derived not from the assessment of educational needs, nor from the nature of the rapidly developing education technology, but simply from the economic dynamics of the situation. The home computer breakthrough occurred in the early 1980s. In 1983 about five million units were sold in the United States, about half of them during the last three months of the year [1]. This comprised a billion dollar industry. Retail sales of educational software in the USA for 1983 began to approach the 100 million dollar mark [2]. Similarly, in December 1983, under the impetus of the Christmas rush, about half a million personal computers were sold in the United Kingdom. By January 1984, there were an estimated 2.1 million homes in the UK owning microcomputers [3].

It is apparent that the next consumer-boom will be in home information technology. Some estimates have forecast that by the early 1990s, the average middle-class family will spend as much on information technology as on the family car. Here are some examples of the sorts of devices the household of the future will contain:

The computer will have its own screen (VDU) rather than sharing the family TV set. The usefulness of the family TV set itself will be extended in three ways: it will have a built-in videorecorder; it will

3

be connected to a vastly extended network by cable television; and a dish on the roof will link it to satellites. Some, perhaps most, areas will be linked by optical fibres, a vast improvement over copper cables: optical fibres facilitate two-way television transmission. This opens the possibility for the family video camera to be used for a whole new range of artistic endeavours and personal communications systems.

To achieve a proper link between the computer and the telephone system one needs a 'modem'. This allows home users to correspond electronically with other people, and to enter massive 'data bases' such as British Telecom's PRESTEL (VIEW DATA). Data bases are electronic information storage systems which have been proliferating around the world. Our householder of the future will tap into a wide range of general and specialist data bases: those used by doctors, lawyers, and other professionals − so-called 'expert systems' which provide information in an easy-to-understand, organized form − often making judgements and recommendations; and others, such as those used by travel agents, theatre ticket agents, and estate agents. Finally, it will become a matter of course to consult, from the home, the more general data bases, such as those provided by the Library of Congress in Washington, other libraries, museums, government archives, etc. In addition, there already exist the computerized data bases provided by the *Financial Times* in London, the *New York Times*, the *Wall Street Journal*, and the *Washington Post*. All these are becoming accessible from the home.

The fact that the *Oxford English Dictionary*, that bastion of scholarship, is being translated into computer form in order to publish its next major revision is indicative of the ascendancy of electronic information systems over the printed word. The reason for translating the *Dictionary* from print into electronic computer pulses is largely economic. It is much easier to edit and revise a work that is on a computer, than a work that is fixed on paper in ink. Because it is easier, it becomes cheaper. If the *Oxford Dictionary* doesn't do it, somebody else will − thereby providing a better and cheaper product.

However, there will be a secondary consequence − in the long run, much more important. The first phase of the revision uses the computer merely as a sophisticated printer. The twelve volumes of the *Dictionary* plus the four supplementary volumes will be integrated, keyed into the computer, then printed out by means of a fast electronic phototypesetter. It is the second phase which is so interesting: the *Dictionary* will be stored in its electronic form as a data base accessible by anyone who has a computer and a device to connect that desk-top computer to a telephone line (a modem). You won't need to buy (and store) 16 volumes of the *Oxford English Dictionary* – all the information contained therein wil be at your finger tips via your computer. Furthermore, you will always have the very latest edition: whereas it is tedious and expensive to print a new revision, it is easy and cheap to change an electronic data base. If Oxford University Press decided to do so, they could introduce changes every day – as soon as they spot a new word in the newspapers, or a new spelling, or merely when they wish to correct a 'misprint' in the dictionary.

The same thing will happen to encyclopaedias. These systems will set the stage for electronic newspapers: the home computer will be coupled to a high-speed printer to obtain a 'hard copy' of the householder's personally designed newspaper. It will bypass the middle man. Instead, it will contain information entered into the system by some reporter, perhaps half-way across the world, only minutes earlier. The householder may be very upset by the latest news, in which case he or she might sit down at the word processor and telex a strongly worded letter in reply. Actually, by the mid-1990s, voice-to-print devices may be good enough and cheap enough for our proverbial householder to talk to the computer, rather than type in the message. In fact the householder, under the stress of the moment, may wish to yell at it, being careful not to distort the vocalization too much, lest the computer, unable to follow the message, misprints it.

Alternatively, a few people may get together to create a short television drama as an editorial comment to be transmitted over the neighbourhood cable television network. If of sufficient quality or interest, it might be picked up nationally – even internationally.

The home computer, coupled to the rest of the home information technology (IT) system, will not only become a vastly expanded family entertainment centre, for many it will also become the home work station. In addition, it will permit electronic shopping for the sick, the infirm, or the just plain lazy, and it will become the home environment control system, automatically adjusting ventilation, heating, lighting, and sound systems to the user's specifications. Home security systems to alert the householder to faulty equipment, fires, or intruders will also become prevalent, including devices to monitor, in the crib, the baby's breathing and heart-beat, particularly during bouts of illness. We shall return to this feature later.

COMPUTERS AND HOME EDUCATION

It should become apparent that computers will become as much a part of our daily lives as did electricity. One of the major impacts comptuers will have on our homes will be a restructuring of the education system. First, as indicated, the computer will provide access to incredible amounts of information stored by the world's leading newspapers, the major libraries, the special collections of museums, government offices, and a host of other professional information providers. In the next century, owning a first-rate encyclopaedia will be as quaint as, today, owning a Victorian slate to scratch on. Second, even more importantly, the home computer will become a personal tutor *par excellence* which, with the help of parents and teachers, will lead to a radical, new home-based education system – *computed-based* education.

Computer-based learning is not suitable for all forms of learning. Playing with a computer is no substitute for playing with children; manipulating buttons on a computer is no substitute for manipulating physical objects like toys or machines; and winning at a game of computer tennis is no substitute for being out on the tennis court. Although computer games can greatly improve hand–eye coordination, they cannot substitute for a whole range of physical activities such as walking or writing. Similarly, although computers can help the development of social skills (for example by simulating

6

social situations) and although a computer may become the focus of special interactions (e.g. when children or adults play on a computer together), by itself a computer cannot replace the normal human interactions required for learning to be human.

Having said all that, the computer is the most important single invention in recorded history. All human activity involving information, including most intellectual activities, will become dramatically improved. We have devised an artificial intelligence external to our brain, potentially of incredible power. Computers will not only help solve problems by extending our brain power outside our heads, they will also vastly improve the information-handling processes going on inside!

By the end of the 1980s, children with home computers will learn to read and write almost as fast as they learn to talk. By the turn of the century, as computer-based education systems will have become well established, twelve-year-olds will have no difficulty mastering the basis of calculus. Our young teenagers of the future will reach comparable levels of understanding in the other arts and sciences as well – the limiting factor being the emotional maturity of the teenager.

There are those who recoil at the idea of three- and four-year-old children reading – of twelve-year-olds, mastering the basics of calculus. Precocious children so often are unhappy and an irritation to those around them. But that is not what we are talking about. It is not the occasional, but *every* normal, four-year-old who will read; likewise every twelve-year-old will understand calculus. The obvious exception will be, of course, brain-damaged or culturally deprived children. However, as we shall see in a later chapter, handicapped children may have the most to gain from computer-based education.

Let's look at it historically. Today's twelve-year-olds could teach Aristotle far more about the physical world than he could teach them. We are not talking about Aristotle as a mature adult dealing with life, ethics, and philosophical considerations which a child may not have the maturity to grasp. We are talking about the natural sciences. Not only does today's child know that the earth is round, have an image of many of the countries and people of the world, know that the earth and the planets revolve around the sun, that the moon is a solid body on which men can walk, that infectious diseases are caused by germs, that the earth is ancient and was once populated by dinosaurs, that the heart pumps blood (not heats it), and many other wondrous bits of information, but he or she could also run rings around Aristotle in mathematics. Today's child, for example, would astound that great mind of antiquity with the concept of the number zero and the whole decimal system based upon that concept. Although, undoubtedly, he would be quick to learn, Aristotle would have to be taught by our school child how to do long division.

TEACHING LITERACY AND LIFE SKILLS

In the popular mind, and among many educators, computers are associated with mathematics, or at least with science, or the computational aspects of other disciplines such as the statistics associated with geography or economics. In contrast, this book will focus almost entirely on the areas of communication and life skills and will outline some of the features of a cradle-to-grave, computer-based education system.

There is an increasing body of evidence that healthy brain development in infants is enhanced by a stimulating environment. We have already alluded to the baby-minding computer which could monitor the infant's vital functions. The computer could be programmed to rock the crib, to provide sounds (including tapes of mama singing a lullaby), to throw patterns of light above the crib, or to move mechanical objects such as a mobile of birds or butterflies. This will never substitute for the actual, continuous, 24-hour, physical contact human babies are entitled to. It will, however, be a great improvement over what babies in Western cultures have been getting since the Industrial Revolution.

At the other end of life one would expect that throughout life one would have used the computer as a sort of mirror of one's personality and of one's world view. Some very sophisticated systems already exist for interviewing prospective employees; these systems use standard aptitude tests which have been converted from a written form into an interactive computer form. They are extremely helpful in providing personnel officers with clues about a potential candidate. Conversely, they can also be helpful to a candidate in assessing his or her own strengths and weaknesses — in assessing interests and desires. They could become a kind of counsellor, not to substitute for other human beings — a friend, a cleric, a teacher — but to present an entirely new feature in our life, a self-analysis simulator. The ability to simulate a wide variety of conditions and to ask pertinent questions would allow programs to be developed which could be extremely sophisticated. These could ask questions such as whether we are afraid of death or whether we are afraid of dying. What might we do to reduce the threat of a painful process of dying? Can we find ways of coming to terms with growing old — with death itself? What keeps us from grappling with these profound problems? Thus, the computer will become part of a genuine cradle-to-grave education system.

TERMINOLOGY

The terms 'hardware' and 'software' are widely used when speaking about computers. The best way to explain these terms is to make the analogy with a record-player: the record-player itself is the hardware; the songs on the record are the software. The computer itself is the hardware; the instructions to the computer comprise the software (see Plates 1A & 1B). Just as a song may be stored on a cassette tape or a record, so may a set of instructions to the computer be stored on a tape or a record (usually a 'floppy disk'). When you play a computer tape in a tape-player and turn on the volume, you can listen to the computer instructions as sound signals. Actually, all you get is a lot of unintelligible bleeps — just as you would have in the early days of radio when you would be listening to morse code. The computer operates on binary code, translating the signals into instructions which may appear on the television screen, or which may end up operating a loudspeaker, a robot arm, a switch to turn up the heat, or, in some way, regulating any number of devices which may be controlled by a computer.

For microcomputers, the 'input' usually consists of the instructions coming from the tape or disk, or instructions typed in by the user. The 'output', most of the time, consists of signals which appear as letters or pictures on the television screen. Actually, the screen may be adapted especially for computer use and be useless for receiving television programmes. In either case, the screen is usually referred to as the 'visual display unit', VDU, in Britain, or the 'cathode ray tube', CRT, in the United States. In this book we will be referring to hardware, software and VDUs. Occasionally, other terms will creep in; they should appear in the Glossary at the back of the book (Appendix D). For example, we have already used the term 'modem'. This is a device which connects the computer to the telephone system.

This book is about computer-based education (CBE). That means we are considering the computer not merely as another piece of education technology, not merely as just another tool. What we are saying is that the entire education system will begin to revolve increasingly around the computer as such a tool. Combined with teachers and parents, books and classrooms, the system over the next few decades will change. At the core of it will be the computer.

The literature is full of terms such as CAL (computer-assisted learning), CML (computer-managed learning), CAT (computer-assisted training), CBT (computer-based training), and others. In general they refer to the use of computers either for administrative tasks or simply as a learning aid for children or adults. Another set of terms relate to the size and capacity of the computers. Three terms in particular, mainframes, minicomputers, and micro-computers may be confusing. The term mainframe refers to the very large computers found in large offices of government, insurance companies, defence establishments, etc. Smaller offices may have minicomputers. What we are discussing for the education system are the microcomputers or, as they are frequently called, the micros. It might be as well to remember that the micros of today are more powerful than the mainframes of thirty years ago. The rate of progress has been such that about every five years there has been a ten-fold increase in computing power. This means that over a thirty-year period there has been a million-fold improvement in computer performance.

We will explore the subject of hardware and software in greater detail in Chapter 4. Similarly, we will explore the other topics introduced above, in later chapters.

Chapter 2
Education and Education Technology

Ethology, the biology of human behaviour, has demonstrated that animals learn in at least two ways. The first is by playing. A kitten chasing a ball looks as though it is playing. In fact, it is learning how to catch animals. The second is by mimicking or, in some other way, interacting with other members of the same species. This can range from mimicking a mating call in birds to hunting behaviour in dogs. In higher primates, more complex behaviour may be learned. For example, chimps have been observed in the wild to strip leaves off a twig and then use the twig as a sort of fishing rod by poking it into a termite mound and extracting termites. The creation and use of such a tool involves learned behaviour.

In human beings, the advent of speech could, in some ways, be considered to be among the first of major education technologies. However, it may be that speech was preceded by miming, dancing, singing, and perhaps other forms of symbolic communication which allowed learning to take place. In any case, the development of an oral tradition in which the elderly would transmit tales across the generations would have helped to develop and maintain successful cultural practices. These must have been among the earliest of human education experiences. By the late Palaeolithic and early Neolithic periods, cave paintings, the use of amulets and sculpture, the general development of art and religion, all must have provided a profound educational environment. The great ancient civilizations evolved systems of formal instruction for rulers, the nobility, and artisans. The appearance of the written word, of books, tapestry, sculpture, stained-glass windows, and church paintings, for example — all of these told stories. All had educational value. They related either to an understanding of the physical or spiritual world, or to an understanding of social behaviour and attitudes.

The Industrial Revolution vastly extended the requirements for education. People working with machinery, engaging in more complex economic interactions needed to know both how to count and how to read and write. Pre-industrial societies were largely ignorant of these matters, and even the nobility, prior to the eighteenth century, had great difficulty being numerate. The early industrial education set out to correct this. However, there were great divides: rich versus poor, male versus female; the roles were hard and fast. There was little chance to cross from one to the other. It is, perhaps, in that early industrial period that there developed the popular impression that machines and numbers are for boys, while sewing and cooking belong to girls. Since the establishment of universal education in the middle of the last century much has happened in education technology: text books, a vast extension of newspapers, magazines, and photographs; in this century, films, radio, records, television, cassette recorders; and more recently in the classroom, overhead projectors, video recorders, and, of course, finally, computers. Of all the forms of education technology referred to above, none were interactive until the appearance of the first teaching machines, and then the computers.

In the 1950s and 1960s, the American psychologist, B.F. Skinner, became noted for providing the research which confirmed that behaviour can be strongly influenced, if not outright determined, by positive and negative reinforcement. That is, if you got hold of an animal, or human, early enough, you could achieve 'correct' behaviour by rewarding it, and suppress 'incorrect' behaviour by punishing it. Skinner was able to use his methods of positive and negative reinforcement to train a wide range of animals. He also had considerable success with certain types of mental patients. And he applied the theory to his own children as well. In a sense he was relying on the classical conditioning, which we associate with the Russian psychologist, Pavlov. If an organism with some in-

13

telligence associated a certain behaviour with a reward, it was likely to engage in that behaviour. If, on the other hand, it was punished for engaging in certain behaviour, then that behaviour would tend to die out. Skinner used this principle to develop teaching machines. In retrospect, those teaching machines seem to have been derived almost directly from his animal experiments. And it may be of some question as to just how useful, and, for that matter, how ethical, they were in being applied to human beings.

The idea of creating interactive programs, where a machine would ask a student questions and the correct answers would be reinforced positively, and the incorrect answer reinforced negatively, is sound in principle. However, in Skinner's teaching machines, the whole system involved drill and practice of a most tedious sort. Positive reinforcement consisted of getting through a program, thereby achieving, what must often have been the delusion of mastering a subject. The negative reinforcement involved failure to do so, and therefore the obligation to repeat the exercise.

That system was not wholly without merit. One of the earliest extensive uses of computer-assisted learning occurred in Ontario in the late 1960s. It was designed to help an innumerate group of teenagers fulfil the maths requirement for college courses. The program was simple drill and practice, but was highly successful. Compared to the more traditional teaching methods, the drop-out rate was reduced by 80 per cent, while staff time dropped to only 10 per cent per pupil. Not the least of the successes was the testimony of a girl who stated that the computer was the first maths teacher who had never yelled at her.

If the teaching machines of Skinner left much to be desired from an educational point of view, they turned out to be a total disaster economically. The machines themselves at today's prices would cost as much as a new car. This meant that only very large and affluent organizations, such as the armed forces, or a few research groups in universities and teacher training institutions, could afford to purchase them. Such a small market meant that there was very little inducement to create for the machines what we would now call software. The programs for such machines were written either by Skinner, or his students, or by a few dedicated individuals. There was no commercial incentive to spend substantial amounts of money. This, in turn, meant that if you bought such a machine you could do very little with it. You would have to spend a lot more money to get programs, and those programs would be very limited. It is not surprising, therefore, that the teaching machines of the 1960s were at least a decade ahead of the technology, were over-sold, and created a negative image of machine teaching. However, Skinner did reinforce the idea that learning could be improved if one had both a proper piece of technology and a proper theory to use with it.

One of the great influences on modern education theory is Jean Piaget, the Swiss education psychologist. Piaget emphasized the biological development of children's brains: that the brain, as it matured, moved through various stages from the time of birth to adulthood.

These stages begin at birth with the basic reflexes: sucking, grasping, crying, and some movement, mostly uncoordinated. Obviously, the human nervous system, at that stage and throughout the 'sensory motor stage', is unable to assimilate and comprehend the basic principles of logic, or even to grasp the more simple insight that objects still exist when they are hidden out of sight.

At the other extreme is the 'formal operational' stage which, according to Piaget, develops during a child's teens as he or she matures into adulthood. One of the major implications of Piaget's scheme and subsequent research is that children cannot be expected to master certain skills until their brain has had sufficient experience, and has matured sufficiently. Although the ages, and the length of each stage may not be quite as precise as Piaget originally defined them, the principle holds: concepts, intellectual skills, and learning capacities usually appear as clearly defined stages. Normally, one cannot bypass any one of these stages, and education must be geared to the maturing brain of the child.

A major step forward in teaching logical thinking in a wide range of mathematical concepts, ranging from Euclidean geometry to Einsteinian relativity, has been provided by Seymour Papert and his colleagues at the Department of Mathematics, and at the Division for Study and Education, at the Massachusetts Institute of

15

Technology. Papert, a student of Piaget, won an international repuation by developing LOGO — a computer language for children (and philosophers). He subsequently gained world-wide attention among educators with his book *Mindstorms: Children, Computers and Powerful Ideas* [1] in which he not only discussed his 'Turtle Geometry' [2] but provided a broad, theoretical treatment of the use of computers for learning. Instead of using the computer to program the child, the child would program the computer. Papert achieved this by giving the child a slave 'turtle' which could be commanded via the computer to move in various ways, and to draw various shapes. This provided the child with the pleasure of controlling an interesting object. The child would begin to explore the world of shapes, space, and the relationships between them. It is probably true to say that no other book has had as much impact on the thinking of computer educationalists. Papert may well be considered to be the father of educational computing.

To Papert, the model of successful learning is the way a child learns to talk, that is to say, a process *without* deliberate, organized, institutionalized teaching. Papert sees the classroom as 'an artificial and inefficient learning environment that society has been forced to invent because its informal environments fail in certain essential learning domains . . .'. These domains include writing or grammar, school maths, and, although he doesn't mention them, probably many other areas found in the school curriculum. Papert believes that the emergence of the computer will produce a great modification of the learning environment outside the classroom: much, if not all, of the knowledge which schools at present try to teach, as he says, 'with such pain and expense and such limited success', will be learned, presumably mainly at home, as the child learns to talk. 'This obviously implies that schools as we know them today will have no place in the future. But it is an open question whether they will adapt by transforming themselves into something new, or wither away and be replaced.'

Papert spent five years at Piaget's Centre for Genetic Epistemology in Geneva. He came away impressed with Piaget's view of 'children as the active builders of their own intellectual structures'. With respect to Piaget's stages, Papert considers the use of LOGO and the Turtle as a most effective means of moving from the 'concrete operational' to the 'formal operational' stage. By programming a physical object, the robot turtle, the child moves from the physically concrete to the abstract and theoretical. Child-like thinking, confined to real objects and relations, matures into the adult-like thinking of formal logic, abstract relations, and imaginary objects or situations. Walking with a turtle along the three sides of a field, is one thing. Thinking about triangles as a class of shapes, is another. Papert conjectures that '... the computer can concretise (and personalise) the formal'. For this reason, the computer '... is not just another powerful educational tool'. It provides us with the means of easing the transition from the concrete to the abstract — from the child to the adult. LOGO and working with the turtle provide the concrete experiences to lay the foundations for 'formal' thought operations.

Papert's book, in our view, should be made compulsory reading at all teacher training colleges and for all educators. It talks about much more than computers. There is, in our view, just one unfortunate aspect: Papert, himself well-versed in mathematics, has devised a brilliant scheme whose greatest (though not only) applicability is in the areas of mathematics and physics. Inadvertently, it has served to strengthen further the image in the popular mind that computers are mainly meant for mathematics and science. It is the function of this book to try to redress that imbalance and to focus instead on the computer as a device for teaching literacy and life skills, to bridge the gap between the sciences and the humanities — which Papert himself calls for.

Chapter 3
The Impending Revolution in Education

INTRODUCTION

The millions of homes with computers comprise a latent force which, once unleashed, will usher in the first genuine revolution in education in over a century. The present system — an extension of the Victorian classroom — will evolve so that it will both return to the privacy of the home, and simultaneously move out into the community.

At the moment, it is the lack of good educational software which is the limiting factor in the spread of home computers. However, this will change during the mid-1980s as we move into the fourth generation of microcomputer educational software packages.

THREE STAGES OF SOFTWARE RUBBISH

The first stage occurred in the mid-1970s as relatively cheap micros first appeared on the scene. Some hardware manufacturers considered the education market as a serious possibility and produced software for it. The result — drill and practice of the dreariest sort. Modelled after the worst features of Skinner's system, it was largely an educational disaster. Only the novelty and the interactive nature of the computer saved the micros from educational oblivion.

The second stage began in the late 1970s. Teachers working with computers began to convert crude drill and practice into games, then moved on to bypass drill and practice altogether as they developed games with specific educational objectives. The problem with much of this material was that it was badly programmed. A push of the wrong button − and the programs would crash.

We are now in the third stage. The age of the amateur is rapidly being left behind as education software publishers combine educational expertise with professional design and programming teams. By creating idiot-proof packages, properly backed up by instructions for parents or teachers, educationally sound games are entering the market at an accelerating pace.

The trouble is that the programs available at the moment, although excellent in themselves, are still ad hoc. No curriculum, no systematic body of knowledge can be built on them. Nevertheless, even with all these limitations, the computer is invading the education system at an accelerating pace.

CHILDREN'S REACTIONS TO COMPUTERS

Table 3.1 illustrates the responses of a child who wrote 'Why I liked the computer' as part of a class exercise. It was, in fact, part of a class report which, under the aegis of the teacher, was to become part of an effort (successful) to raise funds for buying a computer. The original computer had been on loan from our department at Bradford University. It is hard to tell how much of the writing was Emma's idea, how much reflected her peers, how much reflected parental attitudes, and, in particular, how much represented her teacher's influence. Nevertheless, there is much which is typical of the responses computers elicit from children.

There are several interesting features in Emma's thirteen-line treatise. Most profound is the statement: 'I liked it because it did all the writing. All we did was the thinking'. It does raise a number of questions: Was Emma having difficulty writing and did she find typing superior? Did someone else do the typing? What does Emma conceive thinking to be?

Emma opens with: 'I liked the computer because it played games with us'. She picks 'Hangman' as best. This fits in with the report of a Californian psychologist, Thomas Malone. In his study, boys and

19

THE THREE Cs

Table 3.1

EMMA   aged 8   13 May 1982

Leeds

why I liked the computer

I liked the computer because it played games with us
I think the best game was hang man
It helped do my time's tables
The first thing it says is hello then it said
what is your name
So I typed my name
It was very polite
It never got cross
It was like a typewriter with a telly on top
I liked it because it did all the writing
All we did was the thinking
It was like a friend and it's very helpful
There are very exciting pictures

---

girls from Palo Alto (California) also liked 'Hangman', although it came only twentieth out of the top twenty-five games. We must keep in mind that the range of software available to Emma's class in 1982 was extremely limited, so that her comparisons with other games would have been severely restricted.

(A photograph of two boys playing 'Hangman' is shown in Plate 2.)

The liking for computer games is virtually universal. Video games are as popular in Shanghai (see Plate 3) as we know them to be in Sacramento or Southampton. The motivation for play is complex. It must be, at least to a large extent, biologically based. Biologically useful activities activate the pleasure centres. A kitten chasing a ball, enjoys chasing as an activity in its own right. Considering that the kitten will have to make its living as a hunter, chasing is a highly desirable activity. One of the questions computer psychologists need to answer is whether the almost compulsive occupation of boys with computer arcade games reflects their need to develop the hand–eye coordination required of human hunters. Our early ancestors were not blessed with large claws or fangs, but did evolve hunting techniques which involved throwing things, shooting bows and arrows, and using other weapons.

It is interesting to observe the marked sex differences apparent in the enjoyment of certain games. This is borne out in Malone's studies where the game 'Darts' was modified to provide eight different variants. In the original version, a dart aimed accurately by the correct answer exploded a balloon as a reward. This proved to be of greatest interest to boys. However, it was of much less interest to girls. The girls liked the version in which the balloons were popped in another part of the screen and which also introduced music. Malone quotes one girl as saying: 'Darts is more like a boy's game'.

One of our students, Jan Shaylor, tested five educational programs on 9–13-year-olds in schools in Bradford (West Yorkshire). Her results showed that, as one might expect, age was an important factor in determining the acceptability or desirability of programs. What was surprising was that, in this age range, children of only slightly different ages reacted quite differently to the same program. The younger children might find a certain program too complicated, whilst older children found the same program not challenging enough, and therefore boring. One could also interpret the limited results as implying that games had a broader age appeal than drill-and-practice related programs.

All of this is of relevance to educators trying to utilize a computer for instructional purposes. As authors of several educational programs ourselves, it is apparent to us that practice precedes theory. One such program, developed further, and field tested by another of our students (Hilary Swain), entitled 'Letters Learn', found that the delight was not in looking at good pictures, but in pressing the right key and being the person responsible for allowing the picture to be displayed. This phenomenon extends to older people as well. Swain tested out the program on an elderly lady, who was thrilled at being able to work a computer and make things happen on the screen. Unfortunately, most adults still view the computer as a complicated piece of technology, well beyond their competence.

Children do not have such inhibitions. To them the computer is a toy: it is associated with playing games. A four-year-old boy who had never used capital letters, when offered the 'Letters Learn' program was thrilled to bits by the game, yet had no interest in alphabet books at home.

Returning to Emma, an important and typical response of children is her perception of the computer: not only was it ' . . . like a typewriter with a telly on top . . . ' but also: 'It was very polite. It never got cross'. This type of anthropomorphic projection onto the machine is even stronger in younger children. Take the example of a $4\frac{1}{2}$-year-old in the Norton Glebe Infant School in the North-East of England. At the end of the program he read on the screen 'GOOD-BYE MARTIN'. Martin said 'Goodbye'; then kissed the computer. A reasonable hypothesis for explaining this phenomenon is that the computer is interactive, therefore giving the illusion that it is a *being*, rather than a *thing*.

In what is probably the most profound book dealing with computer psychology to date, *The Second Self*, [1] Sherry Turkle analyses the response of children to computers. Turkle has some extremely interesting things to say about the way a child's personality influences how that child relates to the computer. In general, the way a child views the world, the way he or she approaches problems, how a child relates to others – all these determine how a child interacts with computers. For example, two major approaches to the computer involve what Turkle calls 'hard mastery' and 'soft mastery'. Hard mastery involves the imposition of will on the machine. It is the mastery of the planner, of the engineer. Soft mastery is more a conversation than a monologue. It is the mastery of the artist, of the tinkerer. The hard masters delight in abstract schemes and logic; the soft masters in give-and-take. To the hard master, computer quirks are to be fixed and ironed out. To the soft masters, computer quirks are to be savoured – perhaps left in the program as an expression of personality. Hard masters tend to view the computer as a thing; soft masters as some form of being.

Turkle points out that not only may the more science/engineering-oriented children work with computers, but also the more artistic/inspirational children. Because it can be negotiated with, Turkle considers the computer to provide entry for the artistic children into more formal systems. The computer can help bridge the gap between the culture of science and the culture of art – between the hard masters and the soft. This has important implications for sex differences, as well. As Turkle points out, in Western culture '. . . girls are taught the characteristics of soft mastery – negotiation, compromise, give-and-take – as psychological virtues, while models of male behaviour stress decisiveness and the imposition of will'.

We believe that, as computers become widespread in the home and in infant and primary schools, computer-based education will lower the barriers which keep older girls from working with computers and which also keep them from becoming scientists and engineers. In a similar vein, boys will increasingly involve themselves with painting, music, and writing poetry as a result of working with computers. The computer allows them to manipulate sounds, colours, and words, like building blocks. But they will achieve a real quality, only when, as with programming itself, they begin 'living with the object', personalizing it, and through personal experience obtain genuine insight and inspiration.

THE PRINCIPAL ADVANTAGES OF COMPUTER-BASED LEARNING

There are at least fourteen reasons why the computer constitutes such a powerful learning tool:

(1) The most important reason is that the computer is interactive – unlike books, tapes, films, radio, and television, the user determines what happens next. It requires active, motor involvement – it is not a passive exercise. Even if the choices are limited and the program merely provides the illusion of freedom, it still gives children a sense of control.

(2) Computers are fun. Human beings love to respond to challenges, love to make things happen. The computer games industry has grown rich on that basic axiom. By coupling education to games of challenge, computer-assisted learning becomes fun.

THE THREE Cs

(3) Computers have infinite patience. A computer doesn't care if the user responds very, very slowly or how often a child (or adult) makes mistakes. It never gets tired or cranky.

(4) Good education programs never put a child down. Instead they provide effective positive reinforcement.

(5) Computers can provide privacy. Children, or for that matter teachers, can make embarrassing mistakes without anyone seeing them. Ignorance, lack of skill, slowness to comprehend, poor coordination, all can be overcome in privacy. The computer won't tell!

(6) At the same time, the opposite of the fifth reason, the computer can be used to stimulate interactions in a variety of social situations. These include classroom activities involving groups, or a teacher and a single pupil only, or two neighbourhood children, or party games, or a grandparent and grandchild, etc. Many education programs are designed to allow for either individual activity, or for two or more children to play games.

(7) The computers can explain concepts in a more interesting and understandable manner by means of animated material. No amount of talking, writing, or providing diagrams, can compare with making things come alive on the screen.

(8) Whereas it is very difficult to hide things in a book, it becomes possible to hide things in a program which become apparent only on occasion. A book on re-reading holds few surprises (although the reader may have missed points the first time). In contrast, a computer program can be full of surprises. Good programs contain an element of mystery and uncertainty which keep the user interested. It means that the learning experience provides new situations not only for the students, but for the teacher or parent as well.

(9) The ability to simulate complex situations such as chemical reactions, ecosystems, and demographic or economic changes is a particularly powerful reason for using computers in education. Training pilots, managers, doctors, chemical engineers, i.e. any profession or activity where a mistake in the real world could be very costly, is best served by learning on a computer

which simulates the real-life situations. In addition, simulating real events often makes is possible to train students to think 'laterally' across traditional subject boundaries.

(10) The computer allows 'real time', i.e. instant, responses. Whether programming a LOGO Turtle, or transmitting information from one instrument to another across a laboratory bench (or across the world), the computer allows almost instant communication.

(11) This ability to communicate instantly allows a system of pen-pals and colleagues to emerge across the world that is not possible, or never possible to the same degree, by using the post, or the telephone.

(12) The computer can learn from the child. Advanced 'expert systems' learn from the user. One direction of research is to find ways of making expert systems more responsive to students by ascertaining the student's level of competence in a subject, then reacting to the student's questions and answers appropriately.

(13) If a child learns to program, the computer becomes a powerful intellectual tool. For example, computers may be used for doing homework (see Chapters 9 and 10).

(14) All of the above combine to allow a computer to create custom-tailored education for individuals: 'Hello Martin, what shall we do today?' followed by an infinitely patient, friendly, entertaining set of programs, at the right age-level, catering specifically to the pupil's interests, capabilities and needs.

ADVERSE REACTIONS AND CRITICISMS TO USING COMPUTERS IN EDUCATION

Over the years, the authors have either been told or read of a series of criticisms of the use of computers in education, and it may be appropriate to briefly summarize these arguments. They fall into two broad categories: criticisms by people who are not very familiar with computers, and criticisms by people who are. In the former category, one hears the following types of criticisms.

There is insufficient evidence for the effectiveness of computer-assisted learning: enthusiasm, argue the critics, prevails over critical judgement. The history of computers and teaching machines for instructions is strewn with failures and half successes. 'We've heard it all before: teaching machines, slide-tape lectures, video-tape techniques ...'.

Another set of criticisms argues that computers divert and distract from the real job which needs to be done. Other, more traditional, methods are as valid and can be as stimulating and effective as the use of computers. The social and personal context of teaching and learning has been ignored. The extreme form of this argument states that the human dimension has been lost.

A different line of argument, coming from people who have had more extensive experience with computers, is that with limited budgets computers are expensive; you can only afford an occasional one in school. Software is expensive. And most software is rubbish. When you do have good software, it is ad hoc. One cannot cover a whole subject with computers systematically. Finally, such critics point out that teacher resistance is often blamed for lack of progress when, in fact, it is a failure of the technology itself, or the failure to implement the technology properly.

We do not wish to comment on these criticisms in detail, other than to say that the price of computers and software is coming down all the time, the quality of the software is improving by leaps and bounds, and, slowly, whole subject areas will be covered systematically. Criticisms which had validity a short while ago, and even now, will not be valid in the future. The humanistic 'arguments' against computers represent, in the authors' view, a gross misperception of the potential value of computers, providing educators grasp the opportunities which they present. A great deal of the criticism aimed at the use of computers really represents a dissatisfaction with current education – its theory and practice. Computers are seen as extending, or at least perpetuating, an anachronistic system. Instead of favouring the exploratory mode of learning, they provide a sugar-coated version of learning by rote.

Unfortunately, such criticism has a lot of substance to it. However, the fault lies not with the computers but with the software authors. We will have a further look at software in the next chapter. In any case, what should become apparent from the above discussion is that we need to study in depth the impact computers have on children and other users, and also, equally, the reaction of teachers and other educators to the introduction of these devices.

Teachers frequently feel themselves threatened. We have found that some teachers and adults are not only reluctant to touch a computer, but seem aggressively prejudiced against touching it. They don't want anything to do with the beast. However, some teachers at least, may shift attitudes rapidly. One teacher, when she saw the reaction and enthusiasms of the children, lost all her reservations. The computer was taken home so she could try things out for herself away from prying eyes. Eventually she learned to program the computer. The best way to have teachers overcome their fear of being embarrassed in public is, obviously, to allow them to work with computers in private. One solution, much to be commended if the financial resources permit, is exemplified by a small college in Ohio, where the President, Sherrill Cleland, heavily subsidized the purchase of home computers for his staff. The President reported great success: 'The Marietta College faculty are rapidly becoming computer literate. Dialogue at the faculty tables in the campus snack bar is about new computer components that people are putting into their courses. Anecdotes are exchanged about stupid mistakes that they made at home on their computers – demonstrating that our confidence level has grown and we are comfortable in sharing our failures as well as our successes. The mystery has gone out of the computer; it is seen as a tool and not a threat'. Cleland also found a greatly increased dialogue taking place across all the disciplines.

As has been reported over and over again, working with a computer can elicit enormous social dividends. Not only do children cluster round a computer, interacting successfully, but, in fact, so too will adults. Richard Ives, writing in the March 1984 issue of *Educational Computing* has reported on the use of computers in an English as a Second Language (ESL) course. The course was run by the Islington Adult Education Institute. The students, mostly women, comprised a wide range of English ability, although most were above beginner level. Within the course, a dozen first languages, other than English, were spoken by the students. None of the students had any previous experience with computers. A shortage of computers forced students to work in small groups. However, this proved to be an advantage: it provided an intense language environment since talk about computers requires precision in speech. For two weeks, the students had to work out precise instructions for the computer.

The students worked at these tasks collectively. When they did get the computer to respond appropriately, they felt a tremendous sense of achievement. It was not at all unusual for a group to break out into loud cheers upon getting the computer to do what they wanted it to. The course organizer, Helen Bishop, is quoted as saying: 'The computer course ... provided a skill which cannot be practised without communication of a precise and detailed nature. ... it was the computer group whose English improved the most ...'.

SHIFT BACK TO HOME-BASED EDUCATION

The widespread introduction of microcomputers into the home presages the first genuine revolution in education in a hundred years. Our Victorian forebears created a revolution when they decided on mass education. Prior to that, education was for the elite. To teach everyone to read and write was fraught with danger, at least to some Victorians who questioned whether the sons and daughters of working class parents were intelligent enough to learn how to read and write. Others worried that if they did become literate, they would no longer know their station in life. Mass education was indeed a revolutionary business.

Today's classroom is merely an extension of that Victorian classroom. True, it is coeducational, the children stay on into their late teens, they are taught a lot more than reading and writing, and they don't get hit as much. Nevertheless, the present education system is merely an evolutionary extension of that set up a century ago.

During the 1980s there will emerge powerful microcomputer-based education systems which, by the end of the century, will shift much of the education system from school-based back to home-based. Computer-assisted learning (CAL) will mature into computer-based education (CBE).

Grandmothers were humanity's first information storage and retrieval systems. Grandfathers also. However, in those days hunting was a dangerous business. Their mortality rate would have been much higher. Grandmothers were more reliable. Such a view would explain a biological anomaly: why post-reproductive females? The answer: the increased chances of survival for the group as a result of accumulating experience from one generation to the next. Older women had a much more important job to do than having babies: instructing the young in the accumulated wisdom of the ages.

Computers are the most important pedagogic invention since grandmothers. No technology to aid learning, from prayer wheels and medieval stained glass windows to overhead projectors and videotapes, approaches the potential effectiveness of computers — not even books.

HOME-BASED EDUCATION

Even in the absence of computers, there are indications of a slow but significant shift from school-based to home-based education. The most important of these is a Portage Home Visiting Service introduced into Britain to help young children with special education needs. The Portage Scheme was first set up in 1969 in Portage, Wisconsin. It was designed to provide educational and developmental aids to parents trying to teach, at home, pre-school children with mild and moderate learning difficulties. The scheme works as follows. Home teachers visit the families weekly. Together with the parent they identify new skills or areas of knowledge which they would like the handicapped child to learn. The jointly agreed teaching method is written down on an activity chart. It is also demonstrated by the teacher and maybe tried out by the parent with the teacher present. Progress is monitored the following week. Supervisors and professional specialists receive reports from the home teachers, and teachers' staff meetings both help the monitoring process and help to solve mutual problems.

Sean Cameron, of the Psychology Department at Southampton University, has reported the results of two major pilot studies, in Winchester and in South Glamorgan. Parents found that not only did home teachers help them teach their children important life skills, but the teachers also helped with other family problems, such as suggesting management strategies for disruptive behaviour. The home teacher, in fact, usually became an important and respected member of the family. A more quantitative measure of success was to be found in the fact that usually over 90 per cent of the agreed activities were attained each week. An interesting sidelight is that a number of the experienced Portage parents became themselves home teachers once their children had reached school age.

The Portage system not only makes more efficient economic use of scarce professional resources, it also overcomes the current, institutionalized professional/parent dichotomy. The system recognizes that children gain most from education when parents are closely involved in the teaching. This is in marked contrast to those overly professionalized services which loudly proclaim that their function is to help families with a handicapped child, but who actually operate as though the home did not exist except as a source of problems!

Cameron also cites the Court Committee on Child Health Services (1976). The Committee concludes that: 'We have found no better way to raise a child than to reinforce the ability of parents to do so'. Similarly, the National Development Group for the Mentally Handicapped, urged in 1978 that: 'the detailed treatment of mental handicap should largely take place in a child's home in the first few years and gradually others (particularly teachers) should become involved . . .'. Likewise, the Warnock Committee on Special Educational Needs recommended in 1978: 'Greater recognition and involvement of parents wherever possible as the *main* educators of their children during the earliest years'.

The Portage system is designed to help educate *handicapped* children in their own home. However, the special educational needs of handicapped children at one stage, often are the same as the general needs of all children at some other, comparable stage. There is, in fact, a movement in Britain for parents to withdraw their children from the institutionalized education system and provide them with tuition at home. It is true that the number of children involved in this process number only a tiny percentage of the total. Their parents are usually viewed with disdain. However, there are sound reasons for returning to the home, at least a part of the present formal education we inflict on our children. The home is the most important single learning environment a young child has. The computer, with its potential for fun and with its infinite patience will be a most valuable aid to home-based learning systems. As we have already indicated, the next great boom in consumer spending will centre on electronic home information/communication devices.

By the end of the decade, young children working with computers will learn to read and write about as fast as they learn to talk. With further advances in hardware − voice chips, cheap printers, voice to print, voice to voice, cheap interactive video disks, optical fibre links to intelligent data bases, etc. − it becomes likely that by early in the next century, almost all twelve-year-olds will understand calculus and will have reached comparable levels of understanding in science, engineering, geography, history, and anything else that the emotional maturity of young teenagers can handle.

Children will go to school because they need to play with other children, to acquire social skills, engage in sports, go on field trips, fiddle with machinery, perform experiments, dance, put on plays, etc. In short, home will become the place to go to learn − school, where you go to play.

Finally, let us return to grandmothers. Older people are one of the great under-utilized resources of Western society. We should create a new kind of teacher − grandmothers (and grandfathers). The old are a natural for working with computers. Computers require neither strength nor physical ability. They can, however, be a source of enormous stimulation and entertainment. The old also have a natural affinity for the young. Thus retired people would supplement their income by working 10–15 hours a week with pairs of local children at home with the computer. The education system of the future would assure that all children, in their own home, would have a computer system – and a grandmother. Thus, education technology would have come full circle: from grandmothers to computers, and back again.

Section II
Using microcomputers to teach literacy and life skills

Chapter 4
Hardware and Software – an Introduction

The abacus is probably the oldest mechanical calculator known. It has been around in China for a good many millennia. The abacus is a collection of beads on a series of rods or wires (see Plate 4a); the position of the beads in relation to one or the other side of the frame denotes their number. People who regularly work with an abacus, as Chinese shopkeepers do, can attain remarkable speeds in adding and subtracting sums.

It was during the seventeenth century that European civilization reached the point where, since more and more people were spending more and more time manipulating numbers, the need for automatic devices to aid calculations or computations became obvious. Some of the finest minds of the times began to address themselves to the problem: in particular, Napier, Pascal, and Leibnitz.

Napier, as schoolchildren used to know, invented logarithms. That is, he discovered that for every positive number, there exists another number called its logarithm. The relationship between a number and its logarithm is such that the multiplication of any two numbers is achieved by *adding* the logarithms. Similarly, division may be achieved by *subtracting* their logarithms. Napier took this form of mathematics one step further, into the realms of machinery, by creating sets of rods on which the multiplication tables were put in such a way that if you turned the appropriate rod (there was one for each of the ten digits) and added or subtracted whatever numbers came up on the exposed faces, it was the same as if you were multiplying. These rods were referred to as Napier's bones because they rattled around in their nice wooden boxes. They also seemed like magic to the people of the seventeenth century who, for the most part, had trouble adding.

Pascal invented another, quite different piece of machinery. The invention probably related to the fact that his father was a tax-man and must have spent many an hour making the calculations on which he depended for his job. Pascal designed a mechanical device consisting of interlocking cogs, wheels, and axles, which became the world's first calculating machine. You set up the numbers you wish to add by dialling them into the machine, and the act of dialling caused the cogs and wheels inside to rotate appropriately. It was like a mileage counter in the car − only a bit more elaborate. When you had finished dialling in the last number, the result was displayed in a little window. The machine was called the Pascaline, and royalty and scientists alike were astonished. Here was a machine that could achieve what most people had great difficulty doing inside their head. The machine, incidentally, was not a commercial success. In those days, even accountants were so cheap that it didn't pay merchants to buy Pascalines.

Leibnitz improved the Pascaline by introducing a new kind of stepped wheel for multiplication. An ingenious device which, much later, became incorporated into the mechanical and electro-mechanical calculators which preceded the electronic devices we now carry around in our pockets.

By the early nineteenth century, there appeared the grandiose schemes of Charles Babbage. Babbage's theories were brilliant. The trouble was that he was ahead of his time. He spent large sums, initially supplied by the government, then out of his own private funds, to try to produce first the so-called difference engine and then, even more elaborate, the analytic engine. Initially, Babbage's main impact was to improve engineering standards. The multitude of finely shaped cogs and levers required to make the machine work demanded too much of the mechanics of the time.

It was a few more decades before the machine tool industry had advanced sufficiently to allow the production of mechanical adding machines and calculators. These devices began to make significant inroads into manual calculations in the late nineteenth and early twentieth century. Then came electricity to drive the gears and to lay the groundwork for the electronic revolution. Cogs and wheels were replaced, first by electromagnetic relays, then by electronic valves, which were not only vastly superior mechanically, but also could speed up the process a thousand-fold. By the end of the 1940s the first generation of electronic computers had become well established. Three more technical breakthroughs were required over the next three decades in order to get microcomputers into the homes: first the transistor, secondly the development of integrated circuits, finally, when this latter technology had become sufficiently advanced, the etching of the integrated circuits themselves onto small slivers of silicon. The miracle chip had arrived.

It is these last stages which we might look at a bit more closely. Without going into too much detail, the development of the transistor is a fascinating story in its own right. Its theoretical framework can be traced back at least to the 1830s when Michael Faraday observed that the electric conductivity of silver sulphide increased upon heating, while that of metallic conductors decreased. By 1874 Ferdinand Braun, Professor of Physics at Marburgh, had the first functioning solid state device, used subsequently for detecting radio signals. This solid state device, plus Braun's invention of the tuned electric circuit, set the stage for the early radio and wireless industry. Shortly after the turn of this century electronic valves appeared. They were so successful that they eliminated the need for solid state devices. Nevertheless, a few pioneers worked on, intrigued by how things worked and what might be. Among the most important of these was the German physicist R.W. Pohl. By 1933, Pohl knew enough to predict that the electronic valves in radios would, some day, be replaced by small crystals in which flows of electrons could be controlled.

Such crystals were shown to work in the Bell Company Laboratories, New Jersey, on 23 December 1947 by John Bardeen, Walter Brattain, and William Shockley. At that time, Bell Laboratories had mounted a huge operation, and the culmination of a maturing basic science (solid state physics), coupled to the massive investment in research and development, created the transistor. Actually, the state of the art was such that similar work carried out by Benzer, Bray, and Lark-Horovitz at Purdue University appeared to be only a matter of months away from the same discovery. The transistor was recognized as an important breakthrough in electronics: it was tough, it was small, it was light, it used very little power, and for almost all purposes it was vastly superior to the electronic valves − the vacuum tubes − which it replaced. The main problem in those early days, was the difficulty in producing a good quality transistor.

The transistor is a crystal in which small flows of electrons can be controlled to provide signals. It was not long before transistors became highly reliable. The transistor radio helped to initiate the communicative era. It was still made the way radios were always made. You started with a metal chassis and you placed on this chassis, properly insulated, the various electronic components: resistors, capacitors, transformers, etc., including the transistors. You then wired the whole lot together. This was a slow laborious process. By the 1960s, the process was replaced by the integrated circuit. Instead of soldering the wires to various components on a metal chassis in order to connect them, you began with a board made of plastic (or other non-conducting material) onto which you sprayed a pattern of thin strips of metallic conducting material. This created a printed circuit board in which you could then insert the various components. Around 1960, this principle had been refined to the point where you could spray very small, fine circuits onto parts of the silicon slivers themselves. The silicon chip revolution was beginning . . . .

It is not the purpose of this book to go into any greater detail about the history of the microcomputer or how it functions. There are a number of excellent books on the market. We have found very useful Christopher Evans's book *The Making of the Micro: The History of the Computer*. (Other books are listed in Appendix C at the back of this book). What people must be aware of, however, is that the rate of progress is incredible. Chris Evans was fond of saying (in 1978) that, had the automobile industry made as much progress as the computer industry over a thirty-year period, you would be able to buy a Rolls Royce for £1.35, get three million miles to the gallon, and park six of them on the head of a pin. In fact, the rate of progress has been roughly a ten-fold increase in power every five years, which means that, over a thirty-year period, there has been a million-fold improvement in information handling capacity.

This trend in technological advance shows no sign of slackening and will continue well beyond the 1980s. Not only will there be ever more powerful computers and ever more powerful home computers, but the peripherals will also start to come down in price. Such peripherals will include cheap printers, interactive videodisks, light pens, cheap robot Logo turtles, voice chips, and a number of other technical wonders. Coupled with this will be extensive software libraries built up by local education authorities and professional educational publishers. In due course we will have software structured across the entire curriculum and age range, but with enormous diversification. This would allow a parent or teacher to cater to the individual's needs and tastes. There are a number of methods for teaching reading. Some work better with some children than with others. The future holds a wide range of possibilities which will provide a software range as large as the printed material which is available today.

There has emerged one system which, although still expensive, is bound to come of age in the 1990s. This has the following features. First, an interactive video disk (capable of showing between fifty and fifty-five thousand picture frames) is coupled to a computer. These pictures can be called forth either individually or as a series; alternatively, the whole thing can be run as if it were a film. Second, coupled to this interactive video disk is a telex machine which superimposes print on the screen. This permits the teacher, parent, or other user to decide what text to put into the picture, and where. The third component utilizes the computer to put further text, diagrams, or graphics on the screen (this is mainly for the benefit of the producer of the program). Finally, there is a finger-sensitive screen. This allows the user to point by touching some part on the screen thereby causing the computer to respond. There is no need for the pupil to use a typewriter keyboard. He or she may simply point to some aspect of a picture, let's say a complex piece of machinery. Alternatively, one may ask questions, and on the screen there is one box saying 'yes' and another box saying 'no'. The pupil simply touches the 'yes' or the 'no' box. This would also allow for the possibility of translating programs into other languages: because the picture is separate from the text, the text can be typed in any way that seems desirable. At the moment, these systems are so expensive that they are available only to the training units of the armed forces, government departments, or large corporations. However, other systems using a light pen or a 'mouse' are available at considerably lower cost. These systems will be described in a subsequent chapter. What is important is that inevitably the price will come down. When it does, it will put at the disposal of the educator, whether teacher or parent, an incredibly powerful education system – so powerful, in fact, that it will take us some time to catch up with the potential of the new medium.

HOW TO CHOOSE A MICRO

The developments in the technology are moving at such a speed that, although it is easy to buy an *inappropriate* micro, it is now virtually impossible to buy a bad microcomputer. On the other hand, it is equally impossible to buy the *best* microcomputer around because, no matter what one buys, one will find, after a very short time, that there was another one which might have suited the purposes better. Alternatively, it might turn out that the same micro now sells cheaper or has some advanced features. If one waits for the technology to stabilize, one will need to wait a long time. In the meantime, valuable self-development expertise is lost. There is no substitue for hands-on experience. There is no substitute for being able to work with a micro, either in the privacy of one's own home or in conjunction with others in the classroom.

As to specifics, we can only offer some guidelines. The first is: if you are thinking of buying a computer for the home, you should consider which computers already exist in your own family environment. Does the child work on a certain make and model computer at school? Do you or does your spouse use a computer at work? If so, it may be that you should get the same computer at home, because not only will you transfer a certain amount of expertise from school or work to the home, but you will also be able to carry out work that could be transferred from one place to the other. If there are no computers in your family environment, check to see what is being used in the local schools. Do any of your neighbours have them? Talk to them. Buy a few computer magazines; they are now one of the major sections in the hobby field. See what looks interesting. Go to shops, try out a few. Most important, take advice from people who have been working with computers. The chances are it will not be the best advice; however, it is likely to be helpful advice.

In school, the situation is more complex. First of all, there may be no choice, the Education Authority may be committed to certain makes or model. If there is some choice, find out what most kids have at home, find out what other schools have. If you have strong views, do as you like. If not, what do the experts in the education system seem to recommend and, most importantly, why do they recommend the makes or models they do?

Whether at home or at school, the price is often the determining factor. And you may not wish to spend your money only on the computer. You may need a VDU, although at home the television set is usually available. Some computers come with a VDU. Some computers come with a tape recorder. If you need to buy a £25 or £35 tape recorder, some of the price advantages of one make or model turn out to be trivial or actually adverse. Very important is what sort of software is available? And do you want to play the software on tape, or do you want it on disk? Disk drives are coming down in price, but they are still substantially more expensive than tape recorders. And, increasingly, there is the availability of cart-ridges. Software is still a limiting factor. What kind of software is available for your particular needs? All of these considerations will become clearer as you talk to people. Don't be afraid to ask, it is not a sin to be ignorant — only to remain so.

If you have no clear idea of what you want, buy a 'popular' com-puter — the more popular the better. First, a popular computer attracts software companies. Therefore there is likely to be a wider range of software available. For the same reason, there is likely to be a wider range of peripherals such as printers, disk drives, modems, etc. After a particular model has established itself, there tend to arise magazine articles, or even entire magazines, devoted to that particular computer. Also 'user groups', that is, associations of people who own or use a particular computer, tend to spring up around the country. Because of this, such a computer has better second-hand value in case you change your mind, or would like to move on to a larger system.

CHOOSING SOFTWARE

Most shop assistants selling records and audio tapes know very little about the classical repertoire. Whereas they may know by heart the twenty top records for the week in the pop field, their knowledge of classical music can be abysmal. In the early days of the record industry it was even worse: one customer in a provincial city asking for Beethoven's Third Symphony was told: 'I'm sorry we're out of it. But we have the same thing by another composer'. More sophisticated was the response: 'I'm sorry we're out of stock on the Trio you asked for, but we have a Quartet for the same price!'

Though these stories may be apocryphal, the abysmal ignorance of sales staff in most shops today, *vis-à-vis* computer software, is not. If they do know anything about software, it will be games. The most one can hope for is that some shops will let you look at the program on a demonstration tape or disk. As with the early record industry, this will change rapidly. During the transition, parents will need to rely on magazines, friends, neighbours, and teachers for advice. Teachers will have to rely on their advisers, teachers' centres, government information channels, education software libraries, trade journals, magazines, and the representatives of publishers and education suppliers. The last two, although representing a vested interest, do at least make some effort to weed out the worst of the lot and select the better programs. Lucky teachers may have access to good, professional advice.

The first question to ask is: what does the child learn when using this program? In addition to any overt educational objective, is there a hidden curriculum which teaches keyboard skills or hand–eye coordination, or favours socialization. Almost all programs do. Therefore, beware of claims to those particular three. Does the program hold the child's interest? Does it have 'replay appeal'? That is a crucial test. Is the program at the right age level? Most important, at the end of the day, what has the child actually learned? If the entire day has been occupied playing games, was the time spent cost-effective? It is important here not to be too rigid and demanding in setting objectives, e.g. that the child has learned to spell twelve new words or learned the 6-times table. A program that facilitates word recognition, or estimating numbers, may be much more valuable. The main reason for buying a book for a child is for the child to enjoy a story, to enjoy reading, and to become encouraged to read other books – not to learn by heart the meaning and spelling of every new word encountered. So with computer programs. They should provide pleasure as the child explores the world of words, of numbers, of logic, of science, of art, of poetry – or any other aspect of the world.

Good programs never put a child down. They encourage children to express themselves with confidence. Programs must be aimed at the appropriate level of the child's competence: too easy, and the child becomes bored; too difficult, and the child becomes frustrated. In either case, the child will exhibit a negative attitude towards the program.

A program should have built into it sufficient variety and depth to encourage the child to return to the program repeatedly. This will enhance skill development and exploration. Many good programs contain within them several levels of difficulty.

In our view, programs should *not* involve overt violence, nor be racist or sexist. Instead programs should have a global outlook and foster friendly attitudes towards others.

If the above considerations are primary, other considerations are also important. Is the program professionally produced so that it is easy to run and does not 'crash' or contain other programming errors? Does it come with easy-to-follow instructions? Does it explain the educational objectives of the program? Are there other programs to follow on? Is the author of the program, or the company which produces it, respected in education circles?

Programs can have a professional look and sound about them. The imaginative development of graphics, the intelligent use of sound, the documentation, and the packaging itself are good indicators of the professionalism of the production. These are helpful, at times even crucial. But most important is the content. Therefore, before purchasing, run it, read about it, get the feel of it. Although the hardware is still inadequate to allow truly exploratory programs, the emphasis should be on learning by exploration and creativity, rather than on learning by rote. On the other hand, we do need to learn to recognize words, how to multiply, what are the countries in the world and what are their capitals, to identify trees and flowers, fruits and vegetables .... All of these involve memorizing – which may entail learning by rote. Other programs involve practice – practice for children learning to add numbers, for train drivers to follow procedures in emergencies, or for medical students learning to diagnose patients. Therefore, if the program pleases you, and you think it will please the child – go ahead. If you have qualms, see what the reviewers in the computer magazines thought of it. Try to find someone who has used it.

Just remember, in principle there is not much difference between buying a good book and buying good software. The main difference is that book publishing and selling has been going on for centuries. In contrast, the publishing and selling across the shop counter of microcomputer education software began only in the 1980s.

MAJOR PROBLEMS WITH CURRENT MICROCOMPUTER
TECHNOLOGY

In many ways this is a difficult period to get started. The technology has not yet fully matured, and therefore there are many interlocking problems which plague the beginner – and, for that matter, the expert as well. We have already indicated that much of the software around is rubbish. Even what exists is difficult to fit into the existing curriculum. Another problem is the incompatibility between machines. Having purchased a program for one machine at home, doesn't necessarily allow you to play it on another machine in school – even, at times, machines made by the same manufacturer.

An extreme case is exemplified by the problem encountered when series 7 of the BBC model B appeared in 1984. Commercial software produced by Applied Systems Knowledge (ASK) specifically for the BBC model B suddenly wouldn't run on the new series. It seems that a new chip introduced into this model responded differently to a small part of the ASK programs. ASK had not been informed by the manufacturer of the change and found itself confronted by large numbers of irate customers and dealers before replacements could be issued.

Then there are other software problems. Many of the CAL programs in use in schools today ask a pupil questions, then check the appearance of his or her answers. As J.A.M. Howe of Edinburgh University has pointed out, the computer does not make sense of the pupil's answers. It behaves as an idiot savant which accepts a group of symbols, the pupil's answer, and unthinkingly compares it with a stored list of symbols supplied by the author of the program. Unfortunately, some of the pupil's answers are unpredictable, and certainly so are the errors leading to such answers. Other answers are difficult to interpret since such errors may have multiple causes. So there is clearly a limit in the 'intelligence' of the software and the analyses of progress.

The matter is complicated further by the fact that memories on many microcomputers are still too small for many really sophisticated programs which allow maximum scope for children's imagination and creativity.

Another problem is that as the flood of software hits the market, it is hard to know what is available. This is not only true in terms of the publishers or suppliers of such software and where to obtain it, but we have found that even within a school, teachers needing or wishing for certain kinds of programs aren't aware that other staff members have, in fact, acquired such software. Because there is no satisfactory storage and retrieval system as yet, and because there is no proper library classification system, it is difficult to know what software is available and how to obtain it.

THE THREE Cs

Jan Shaylor, one of our Ph.D. students is working to develop a disk-based program to help schools file (and find) their computer software. Another approach to classifying education software is exemplified by a paper presented to the 1984 Educational Technology International Conference by Dr Gordon Mills, Senior Lecturer in Micro-computer Applications in Psychology at the University of Bradford [1]. His approach is summarized by Table 4.1. Mills classifies education software in terms of the amount of control exercised by the learner.

Table 4.1

Learning Mode	Type of Software
– – – – – – – – – INSTRUCTIONAL	Demonstration/textbook mode Drill and practice Programmed learning – linear mode Programmed learning – branching mode
– – – – – – – – – REVELATIONAL	Educational games Case studies and simulations
– – – – – – – – – EXPLORATORY	Problem-solving Creative activities, e.g., LOGO
– – – – – – – – – EMANCIPATORY (Utilitarian) – – – – – – – – –	Maths packages (e.g., stats/spreadsheets) Word Processing Database Packages

LIVEWARE PROBLEMS

The main problem, however, is not with the hardware or the software, but with the liveware. That is to say, the major problem is the lack of trained teachers, administrators, and parents. Worst of all, there is a lack of basic research into the whole process of learning. Not only do we not have fully comprehensive theories of learning, but we have very little information on how these theories work when using computers.

The lack of trained teachers is probably the major limiting factor in preventing the rapid spread of computer-assisted learning in schools in the mid-1980s. Many teachers are so frightened of computers that they never find out how easy it is to run one. This fear often reflects their mathophobia.

The fact that they daily engage in activities much more complex, such as cooking, or for that matter, using a typewriter, is not generally understood. Teachers desperately need hands-on experience — not to learn how to program a computer, but simply to learn the skill of turning it on and off, and how to load a program and run it. It is a skill which can be taught in a matter of hours, if not minutes.

Unfortunately, many teachers outside of science and maths have an image of themselves as technological incompetents. Yet they have no trouble driving a car. Their image of themselves is distinctly wrong. As discussed in a later chapter, we need to develop ways of overcoming these psychological blocks. The real problem is to know what to do with a computer once you know how to run it. This may require a much broader education base for the teacher.

Administrators often don't seem to realize the importance of computers in education. They don't seem to comprehend a revolution has begun. For this reason they won't provide teachers with time off in order to learn about the subject. Nor will they provide them with the proper resources. Such resources include not only computers, printers, and other peripherals, but also a steady budget for purchasing software, periodicals, and a travel budget. Teachers need to talk to other teachers across the country in order to compare notes and improve their own level of computeracy.

Lastly, many parents are not only often wholly ignorant of the potential of computers but, worse, have very little grasp of modern educational thinking. The generation that comprises today's parents grew up in an education system still heavily dominated by a pristine Victorianism. The predominating attitude may be caricatured by the adage 'it doesn't matter what you teach them, as long as they don't like it!' Parents are still very much in favour of memorizing by rote, timetables, and rules of grammar, and, as such, are often *the* impediment for developing enlightened education software for the home market.

Finally, basic research into educational practice, although it has moved substantially in the second half of this century, clearly has a long way to go. Undoubtedly, this lack of progress and insight reflects the fact that we understand so little about the functioning of the human brain. Some call this the last great frontier in the biological sciences. In part this research will be aided greatly by the development of advanced artificial intelligence systems using computers. Artificial intelligence research stimulates understanding of the brain, just as understanding of the brain stimulates progress in artificial intelligence. As our understanding of the development of the brain increases, so will our understanding of the processes which children undergo as they learn. Undoubtedly, the expanding use of computers as a learning aid will provide new insights into the learning process and will, by early in the next century, increase the efficiency of the learning process to undreamed-of levels.

USING THE COMPUTER FOR ADMINISTRATION

For many years very large schools with thousands of students and a staff of several hundred could work out a timetable only by using a computer. Now more and more administrative tasks are being undertaken by computer. Files of students, names, addresses, and marks achieved, are kept more confidentially on a computer disk than in a filing cabinet. Duty rotas, details of clubs, and use of rooms can be dealt with by computer. The word processing facility is vital for a secretary faced with the prospect of sending identical letters to hundreds of parents. The list is endless. Statistical forms which appear with unrelenting regularity can receive their data from the computer program.

Essentially the computer is being used in schools' administration the same way it is being used in business offices, hospitals, banks, etc. It can be used as a convenient record-keeping device; it can be used for manipulating more complex interrelated pieces of information such as timetabling. A more sophisticated use is computer-managed learning (CML) or CAMOL (computer-assisted management of learning), which keeps track of pupils' progress. With monitoring systems such as readability scores, the computer will also undoubtedly prove to be most helpful. If they do not exist already, it should be fairly easy to devise computer programs which assess readability score. Such a program would allow an educator to type in a passage. The computer would compare the words in the passage with a standard word list (e.g., such as one provided by Dale, or revised by Stone) which are the realtively 'simple words'. Such a comparison would show how many 'difficult' words there are in the passage. The computer could also count the average number of words per sentence, and count the number of syllables per hundred words. On the basis of these three criteria, it could provide a readability score which relates to the reading age. Thus it becomes possible to administer certain tests much more readily using computers. This would become part of a monitoring system to keep track of a pupil's progress.

In the future CML will become almost unnecessary if most of the pupil's work is done on the computer. It would be easy, using the computer, to monitor which games or programs the child was working with. The computer could also ascertain at what level of difficulty the child was working, including the child's accuracy and speed.

Although all of the above will be an aid to educators, the use of computers in the administration of education, including monitoring pupils' progress, constitutes merely a technological advance no greater than the introduction of electric typewriters into offices. Although not trivial, it is not going to be revolutionary. Therefore that is not what this book is about.

Chapter 5
From Babbling to Spelling

'Children learn to use language through their experience of language as it is used by other people and through the expectations of using language other people have of them' (Joan Tough, *Talking and Learning* [1]).

PRE-TALKING

An experienced parent can usually tell by the way a baby cries exactly what is needed: whether it is food, loving, changing, etc. Whilst engaged in these activities, parents usually talk to the baby, sibling, or another adult. It is the sound of the voice as much as the activity which soothes baby and helps create a feeling of security. The conversation which takes place during the ministrations is not monosyllabic, rather it is a continuous sound of the human voice. Talking and singing is recognized as being essential for the well-being of every young infant.

There are occasions when a baby cries for no apparent reason. Parents who are busy or tired (especially during the night) become angry, frustrated, and guilty at not being able to settle the crying babe. A vicious cycle develops. An angry parent is the person least likely to settle a fractious infant. With the advances being made in microtechnology it should be possible to create a soothing calm situation by means of subdued lights, human voice patterns, and cradle rocking. This would settle the baby and allow the busy parent to carry on with work or a tired parent to go back to sleep.

As the child grows, a caring parent speaks more and more frequently. Even though the only response is a smile there is a growing awareness on the part of the baby that sounds have meanings, sounds can soothe. We know of a girl of six years of age suffering from hydrocephaly who could only be stopped from moaning by having music played to her or having her parents talk to her. It was extremely wearing for her parents and she was institutionalized.

The future 'cradle-computer' system would contain the following elements. A microphone is placed in or near the crib. The computer would contain a chip to analyze the sounds coming from the crib, including the equivalent of a voice-to-print device. Depending on the sounds emanating from the baby, the computer would activate a variety of devices, depending also on various schedules during the day or night. Minor distress signals during the night would activate a cradle rocker and/or mother singing a lullaby (with or without musical background). Serious distress signals would be transmitted to the parents.* During the early morning, or at other appropriate times, the computer would project light patterns onto the walls and ceiling, as well as play music. Ever alert to

---

* The cradle-computer system would not only enrich the baby's environment, providing entertainment, hence education, it would also act as a health and safety monitor. Using the principles developed in hospitals for continuously monitoring critically ill patients, the cradle-computer could alert parents the instant it detected the infant to be in serious physiological or psychological distress. Cot deaths and fatal accidents could be virtually eliminated − certainly if the cradle-computer system were to be coupled to a medical-expert system instantly available on the computer to parents who, as part of their education, have been trained both in the principles of first aid, and how to use a medical-expert system properly. While the parent started on a life-saving routine, a simple command shouted to the computer, whose alert to the parents would have switched it onto 'emergency mode', would activate the medical services of the community. For example, a 'nine-nine-nine . . . Medical Emergency' call, would contact both the physician on duty, and the para-medical ambulance crew. The physician would read the computer's monitor and talk to the parent. He or she would then decide on whether, and what kind of medical team to send with the ambulance. The physician would also back up the medical expert system, providing reassurance and further suggestions while the ambulance was on its way. The system could be extended by the use of a video camera, connected via optical fibres to allow the physician to actually see the baby, as well as talk to the parent and observe the computer's sensors. Needless to say, such an electronic medical service would apply to all members of the household, but it would be particularly valuable for infants and old people.

the child's vocalization, the computer would respond to various moods and, in due course, to the child's verbal commands. The computer would also be connected to a variety of computer-controlled toys − not by wire, but by remote control systems − which the child would learn to activate by emitting certain calls or commands. These could include a variety of rattles, rolling balls, dancing teddy bears, moving turtles, birds flying around on a mobile, etc. As the infant grows older, the nature and diversity of sounds change. The voice-to-print chips now cause the computer to respond visually to the kinds of sounds produced by the baby. For example, the visual shapes could mimic the shapes of the mouth emitting the sound. The colours or the brightness could depend on the loudness. Letters, phonemes, or words could appear on the screen. For the time being, the patterns would have no significance for the infant. Later, however, they would comprise the sort of experience which would reinforce the early reading and writing programs.

When the infant babbles, coos, and gurgles, it is engaging in vocal experiments. The sound of its own voice provides feedback. Using the computer for a limited time each day would provide visual feedback as well, thereby reinforcing vocalization. This would provide an additional stimulating environment − to some extent under the control of the infant. Some of the time the visual patterns may be put on at random, not related to voice. At other times, the visual displays should be switched off so that the baby's brain would concentrate on *listening* to the sounds coming out of its throat.

Normal children love to listen to people talking. John Holt, in his book *How Children Learn* [2] has stressed that 'Children like hearing adults talk even though they can't understand much or most of it'. Babies as young as six months turn in the direction from which the sound emanates. Gradually there is a realization that sounds are a means of communication, of getting what is wanted, or attracting attention. With what joy are the first sounds towards recognizable speech greeted. Encouragement and praise are lavish so baby realizes the importance of verbal communication. Even though a parent communicates in sentences, a baby begins to build a spoken language one syllable at a time. Early utterances are monosyllabic. A toddler who can speak in phrases at 18 months is regarded as being advanced for its age. On the other hand, a child who lives in a non-communicating household has its language development hindered. A deaf baby does not learn to speak as it is not aware that sound has any meaning or significance. Parents teach their children words, particularly nouns by pointing and naming 'cat', 'dog', etc. The meanings of conversations or requests are often misunderstood if a child has not already built up an understanding of the words and phrases being spoken.

Just as a child is encouraged to talk by being praised, so is behaviour also controlled by the interaction of the child with an adult. When a child is found in a dangerous situation, e.g. near a fire or climbing stairs, the behaviour is controlled by the tone of the voice as well as by the words which are spoken. One of the first words a child learns is 'No'. It delights in the consternation and frustration this negative answer creates in an adult.

A very young child coming into a room does not see individual items in that room. It sees the whole room as a continuum. An adult is needed to draw attention to a particular item for the child to be able to focus its eyes on it. This is a prerequisite to learning the name of a particular object, whether it is a toy, a chair, food, etc. The insatiable curiosity of a child will automatically draw its attention to interesting objects or shapes without the child needing to know the name of the object. A great deal of adult-child interaction can take place at this stage.

Before the age of ten months, if an object is hidden from a baby, it is forgotten. Gradually the baby realizes, by constant repetition of the 'game', that the toy dog still exists when it is hidden behind the cushion and when it is so hidden the infant will move to retrieve it.

TALKING

The insatiable curiosity of young children can be very wearing. Initially, in the non-verbal stage, the child moves around a room touching, moving, holding objects. It has to be continually supervised. A computer program showing a mix of novel and familiar objects and sounds can hold the attention of a curious child for a considerable period of time.

When a child begins to ask questions, the experience can be frustrating both for child and adult if the adult attempts to give long, detailed explanations. A child's 'mind' vocabulary has not yet assimilated many of the adult words and phrases. Simple one-sentence explanations are sufficient to satisfy the majority of children. Children below the age of three can soak up a remarkable amount of knowledge if they are in a stimulating environment, but they need words to help make sense of their environment.

When a child sits on its father's knee for a story, as the book is read, the child looks at the pictures and words. At first the words and pictures will have no meaning. Just as in the real world a child has to learn the names of objects, so in the world of books a child comes to realize first of all by the pictures and then by the words, that different books present different stories. Inevitably, favourite stories are requested and read and re-read until the child's memory of the story is word-perfect. Should a tired adult make a mistake, it is quickly corrected by the child. Nursery rhymes, traditional stories, stories mirroring their own lives, stories for fun, repetitive stories, all are essential at this stage.

Computer programs of stories are invaluable at this stage. Unlike books they can keep the element of surprise or the punchline hidden until the end. When very young children are first introduced to books they do not understand the importance of beginning at the beginning. They turn the pages over randomly. Computer programs can gradually unfold a story. In addition, something can be kept hidden for another day.

Computers can increase a child's interaction with other people; children at this age cannot sit soundlessly looking at books, objects, or computers. A running commentary is obvious throughout any activity. A computer generates a great deal of interaction: in one of our own programs, 'Words Words Words', the movement of the bus from one scene to the next encouraged children in class to talk about their own experiences of bus journeys; while the ghost flying over the castle produced squeals of mock fear. In Michael Holt's 'Let's Count' the music of the 'Drunken Sailor' encouraged children to sing together while, when they made a mistake, the 'raspberry' produced giggles. (See Plates 5 and 6.)

No-one is quite sure when a child begins to realize that printed words have a meaning. Teachers and parents can hasten this realization by pointing to words as they read the story out loud to the child. Once a child reaches this realization the process of learning to read has begun. An important point to be noted is that children learn to read familiar words or phrases easily if they are within the framework of their 'mind' vocabulary. It does not matter whether the word has three letters as in 'cat' or eight letters as in 'elephant'. If it comes within their frame of reference it is recognized and 'read'. The more children are exposed to a wide variety of stories, either on film, in books, or on computer, the greater their reading vocabulary will become.

Once this stage is reached a computer can be of incalculable value. Programs should contain words, scenes, sentences, and stories familiar to the lives of small children. Incidents of everyday life, meals, playgroup, shops, home, etc., if they are presented in a colourful and interesting way, as with familiar story books, will be repeated over and over again.

Children also need stories to help them cope with feelings and emotions. Feelings of jealousy and anger can be frightening to a small child. Presented in story form, either in books or on computer, they can be brought to the realization that everyone has these feelings – that these feelings pass, and that these feelings can be controlled. *I hate my Teddy Bear, There's a nightmare in my cupboard, Come away from the water Shirley*, and many more, are books which deal with emotions young children feel, along with the traditional *Three Bears* and *Little Red Riding Hood*. They are all enjoyed by young children, helping them towards a greater understanding of themselves and children around them.

As the technology advances, and more sophisticated computer programs come onto the market, there will be stories or situations which can be controlled by the children. Using the computer, they can work through their emotions – fear, jealousy, excitement; they can experience these feelings 'secondhand', i.e. through the children or animals named in the story. Each child can put in his or her own name and so experience these feelings but cope with them in the safety of sitting with a computer. There can always be a happy ending to the story — but it will be the child's *own* story!

Research has shown, e.g. The Oracle Project and Michael Armstrong's *Closely Observed Children* [3], that children's language and reading skills improve dramatically when they have the frequent attention or even just the presence of an adult. Work and behaviour patterns are much more meaningful. The presence of an adult helps a child keep control of a situation. Can a computer replace this adult? In certain circumstances it can. An adult can start to work through a program with a child initially. Once it has become familiar, the program can be left running and the child will feel confident and encouraged to work through the program alone or with other children. Using a number of programs at this level should improve the vocabulary quite dramatically, as the same words or phrases will appear and re-appear in a variety of settings, while at the same time the computer will be replacing the adult who normally has to help at this stage.

No matter how sophisticated and interactive micros become, they will never replace human physical contact. Constant human contact, much of it physical, is essential to the well-being, security, and development of all children. Children need loving, cuddling, and stroking. No computer can ever replace the human touch, but it can help alleviate the heavy demands a young child places on a parent.

It is an enormous advantage if more than one child works through a computer program at the same time. Children need to talk to build up their spoken vocabulary. The computer provides an ideal focus for talking it out with peers. The same child can play several roles while using the same program: initially, as the learner being helped to work through a new program; then a more equal role, working through the program a second, or third time; finally, a teaching role, showing another child how to work through the program. This last role is invaluable for a shy child who lacks confidence.

In contrast, watching children working in the sand, or at the painting or modelling table, it is noticeable that although they do a great deal of talking they are not necessarily talking to each other. If they do talk to each other, the conversation does not follow on as in adult conversations. In contrast, a computer program sparks off a dialogue between two children. The pictures, scenes, and words provide a focus for their eyes and hands, but most of all for their minds. The mechanics of pressing the keys can give rise to further areas for discussion or argument.

PRE-READING

When a child can read easy phrases and sentences, computer programs can be a direct means of helping it to recognize that sentences are made up of words, and that words are made up of letters. Many parents still believe today that learning the alphabet first and building up words phonetically is the way children learn to read. The opposite is true in most schools. As mentioned previously, children learn familiar words and phrases and only gradually learn letters.

One of the great advantages of computer programs is their versatility. As indicated above, different parents or teachers prefer different approaches to the teaching of reading. Different children respond differently to different learning situations. We agree with Frank Smith's dictum: '*children cannot be taught to read*. A teacher's responsibility is not to teach children to read but to make it possible for them to learn to read' [4]. Smith also considers that: 'In the two-thousand-year recorded history of reading instructions . . . no-one has devised a method of teaching reading that has not proved a success with some children' [5]. Computer programs, authored by those who have a genuine insight into the process, can provide any number of alternative routes to help children learn how to read.

One complication which can be over-emphasized in working on a computer is the difference between upper and lower case letters, i.e. capital versus small letters. The use of the Qwerty keyboard on micros caused many teachers anxiety. They feared it would lead to confusion and that children would use capital letters more when writing their own stories. Children are far more adaptable than we give them credit for. They readily accepted, in fact did not notice, that the Qwerty keyboard contained capital letters, while up on the screen, they read words and sentences presented in the conventional manner, using lower case letters. Again to quote Frank Smith: 'Adults often underrate the intellectual achievements of very young children in mastering language ...' [6].

Once children come to the realization that words are made up of letters, they being to learn to spell. However, this is usually incidental to meeting the same key words in many different contexts. That is, most are more interested in recognizing the word than its letters. So it can become hard work to teach the rules of spelling, the endings of verbs, changing of tenses, phonemes, etc. Interesting computer programs are being developed as aids to spelling to replace the dreary spelling test every Friday afternoon which so many children learn to expect. Parents like to have their children bring home lists of spellings to learn. The ensuing drill and practice makes parents feel that they are helping with their child's education.

Home computers will gradually take over this role and so relieve both child and parent of this educationally dubious practice. Programs like 'Words Words Words', 'Children from Space', and, as an early introduction, Gloria Calloway's 'Hide and Seek', help children both with spelling and with the realization that there is a direct correlation between words and pictures on the screen. In the same way that having a story read by an adult from a picture book helps, so good computer software can help children both at home and at school to come to the realization of this link.

READING

Once children reach this level of intellectual achievement, heavy demands are made on adults as a youngster needs to have someone who can hear them read. Hearing a child read a story requires patience and skill. Patience to sit and listen to stories over and over again. Skill to know how and when to intervene when reading mistakes are made. Many parents think the correct way to help a child to read an unfamiliar word is to spell it out phonetically. This leads to confusion and frustration. Confusion because the English language is confusing. How do you spell out, phonetically, such words as 'two', 'through', and 'here'. To teach such words takes time and in many cases there are no set rules which cover particular words, e.g. here hear, read reed, where wear.

The limiting factor in reading, as Frank Smith points out, '. . . is not the rate at which the visual information gets to the eye but how long the brain takes to make its decisions' [7]. Children (or adults) learning to read must not be overloaded with new information. For example, to comprehend a word they must not have to spend time deciphering various letters (as with reading a note written by someone with bad handwriting). The vast majority of words must be words which are easily comprehended by the reader; and the few unknown to the reader should be in such a context as to be easily deciphered.

When children are reading they need to understand what the story is all about. To have a pause to spell out a word breaks the concentration needed to understand the story. Therefore an adult hearing a child read should tell the child what the word is which is causing the problem. If the book is at the correct reading level for the child the unfamiliar word will be repeated many times until it becomes a familiar one. The heavy reliance placed on reading schemes in schools is one of the answers to the problem set out above. Any reading scheme, whether it is 'Ginn 360' or 'Dragon Pirate', presents new keywords gradually but still sufficiently frequently to allow such words to become familiar.

There is a need for a series of computer programs to help with this stage of literacy development. Ginn and Longman have already attempted to do this, and the ASK programs under development also present a seriated reading scheme. Just as there are many reading schemes in schools now, so will there be many computer programs to cover every aspect of reading development.

The important advantage of computer software has over conventional reading schemes is its versatility. Programs can be altered to suit individual requirements. The whole story is not revealed at the first reading. Traps and tricks can be built into the program to help in the intellectual development as well as the reading development. 'Grannies Garden' by 4mation is one such program. The children have to think and remember where they fell into traps and, on repeating the program, avoid the dangers in order to emerge victorious at the end. The personal involvement is evident and the build-up in excitement and satisfaction encourages young users to return again and again as though to a favourite book. Older children, in contrast, may lose interest once the program is completed and, like a picture puzzle that has been finished, never want to see it again.

As mentioned previously, an important advantage of computers is the possibility for an active involvement of more than one child.

Usually reading is a solitary activity. Once a child has begun to read, apart from reading aloud to an adult, the book is usually read quietly at home or at school. Under these circumstances it is not easy to check that the story has been understood, other than by asking questions, or having the child write a précis. Both exercises can be boring and can lead to a young reader not wanting to read. Here again a computer program can have the edge because, unless the child understands and gives the correct response, nothing happens. Working with other children means that a discussion can take place. Pros and cons of any given situation presented on screen can be argued. This social interaction leads to a satisfactory conclusion both in terms of finishing the program and working with other people.

A national Opinion Poll published in April 1984 pointed to the sad fact that very few children at the age of 10 years read for pleasure. In other words the education system of Great Britain, even with the help of parents, does not succeed in getting children to read voluntarily. It is *sad* because many children are missing out on a vast store of information and pleasure available in libraries and bookstores. It is *serious* because a lack of reading enjoyment hinders the build-up of higher reading skills which are vital to students going on to further education. Computer-based literacy programs, properly used, will generate an interest in reading which

at present, is lacking. Computers, unlike books, are interactive.*
In addition, good programs contain hidden extras, and computers
foster social interactions. Is it the solitary nature of the reading
activity which prevents children from picking up a book? If so, then
a good computer program is definitely the answer. As the
technology improves, so will the ability of the software publishers
to generate interesting and exciting reading programs. These will
turn the children back to the written word and reinforce the keen interest shown by children of six and seven years of age.

---

* Interestingly, since the advent of computers, a few books have appeared which allow some
interaction. These give two or more choices at the end of some of the pages to allow the child
to determine different story lines.

Chapter 6
Reading, Writing, and Comprehension

'One essential skill of reading that no reader is ever taught is to depend upon the eyes as little as possible' [1]. Frank Smith reminds us that this issue is fundamental to the teaching of reading. Unless children have a good working vocabulary, i.e. the ability to relate events, recall happenings, discuss details, and understand what their own world contains, they will not learn to read. The ability to match words that are written, with words that they can understand is vital. Children can easily understand the printed words 'I like playing with my friends' because they picture themselves playing with their friends. However, such children would not be expected to read and understand 'J'aime mes amis' unless they were bilingual or French. The 'non-visual reading' as described by Frank Smith can only be improved by building up not just the spoken vocabulary of children but the 'mind vocabulary' of children as well. This can only be accomplished by allowing children to experience many different scenes and situations. A school building is not necessarily a good place for this to happen. It is certainly not the only place.

Obviously when a child first starts school it is new and exciting. Many new experiences are encountered and new words are added to their 'mind' vocabulary: 'I am playing with bricks', 'We are going into the playground', 'It is time for dinner'. Peter, who had only started school, was asked by his teacher, 'Have you read today?' Peter was quiet for a while, then replied, 'I have a little bit of red on my jumper'. A girl of four and a half, attempting to describe another girl said: 'You know, the one with the sponge on her head'.

The 'sponge' was a hair bun covered by a pink hair net which was Jessica's new hair style. These examples illustrate the process of building word consciousness in children first starting in school.

Children who have difficulty with reading or who 'switch off' from reading are those who have been forced to read beyond their comprehension level. When reading aloud to an adult the words do not flow fluently but are stilted and haltingly read, and when questioned on what has been read there appears little or no sign of comprehension.

Reading begins to coordinate the written word with the mind vocabulary. That is how what is read is understood. It can be a slow process. One of the most successful ways of teaching reading is to write down a story dictated by a child on a particular topic, e.g. My Mum, My Home, School, etc. This 'story' can be built up to form a book.

Using a computer, the 'book' referred to above can look professional. Very young children can be taught the Qwerty keyboard by using programs such as 'Letters Learn' or Don Walton's 'Cat 'n Mouse'. Once that is accomplished a very young child is able to write a story, using a computer as a word processor. Such a story need only be one sentence long. Printed out with a drawing above it on the 'print-out' sheet, it is eagerly read by its author over and over again. Each day, the story can be added to, either at home or at school. 'A word processor provides as many possibilities as a pen with the additional advantages of clarity, compelling redrafting facilities and the fascination of a screen medium' (Don Clark, *A World in a Grain of Sand* [2]). An example of the work of a seven-year-old in an average school is presented below. A picture of children working with a word processing program is shown in Plate 7.

VOCABULARY BUILDING

Once a child is reading with comprehension, fluency develops rapidly. At this point, it is important for a wide variety of experiences to be shared by a child or group of children with a sympathetic

THE THREE Cs

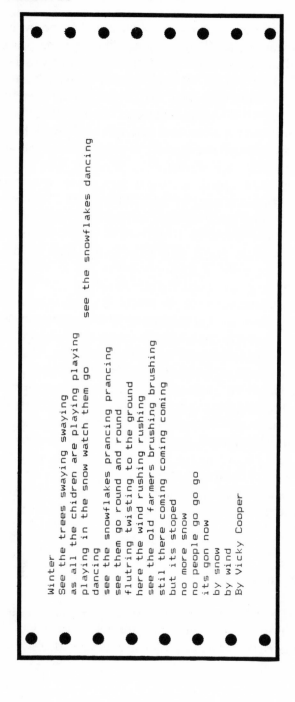

Winter
See the trees swaying swaying
as all the chidren are playing playing
playing in the snow watch them go   see the snowflakes dancing
dancing
see the snowflakes prancing prancing
see them go round and round
flutring twisting to the ground
here the wind rushing rushing
see the old farmers brushing brushing
stil there coming coming coming
but its stoped
no more snow
no people go go go
its gon now
by snow
by wind
By Vicky Cooper

adult who will stimulate conversation, help with new words, and present a varied environment. In a stimulating environment, a child's vocabulary will expand and develop. Children love strange, unfamiliar, funny, or long words and will repeat them over and over again. Once road signs, advertisements, and shop signs have been learned and understood, a young child will read them with relish every time they appear. Very young children quickly realize that they can find out what is on TV by turning to a particular page of the newspaper to find out when *Tom & Jerry* or *Sesame Street* is being shown. Coupled to all this reading is a child's sense of achievement − a sense that it is entering the secret world of the grown-ups.

Spoken, written, and reading vocabularies need extending simultaneously for maximum achievement; but obviously spoken language far outstrips the other two because a child hears it from birth. Reading vocabulary develops next in the form of familiar books and computer programs.

Teaching reading involves a process of filling the brain with increasingly complex *structures of organized information* which allows the individual to rapidly decipher letters, syllables, words, phrases, sentences, and finally concepts. There is a hierarchy of information patterns leading from letters to sentences. Knowledge represents a matrix of organized information. Knowing how to read at the sentence level is an example of 'knowledge'. Such knowledge in turn may become part of a further hierarchy leading to profound insights and concepts. Learning to read simple sentences is a matter of 'training'. Learning to understand the concepts conveyed by complex sentences, paragraphs, articles, and books is a matter of education. The boundary between the two is not clear. Reading simple sentences is a matter of training, whereas reading with comprehension becomes a matter of education.

WRITING

Writing is the most difficult skill to learn for a young child. Many adults cannot remember how they felt when learning to write. One of us (CC) vividly remembers being given a small lined book in which her teacher had written 'OOO . . .'. She was told to fill all the

65

lines with these strange symbols. She quickly became bored and began to convert the letters into faces by putting in eyes and mouths. The response of the teacher was to administer a caning for failing to carry out instructions.

Children of 5 years start school. Consider what they have to do to learn how to write. First they have to think of what to write. This can be hinted at by the teacher. Then, they have to have pencil and paper. Perhaps the pencil needs sharpening! They have to learn how to hold the pencil correctly, learn to write from left to right – remember to put spaces between the words, and struggle to write in a straight line (lines on the paper do not help) .... The list of difficulties is endless and yet teachers insist, parents insist – pressure is inescapable – so the five-year-old struggles to please. To leave the teaching of writing until the age of seven is no help. The process is still the same.

Teachers and parents today begin by writing a word or sentence to be traced over. Later a child is encouraged to copy underneath the adult's writing. Finally a child begins to write his own stories. As previously mentioned, a story is as long as one sentence, half a page, two pages, or whatever length is deemed necessary to express thoughts and retell events in print. The word processing facility of the computer greatly enhances this story writing. Once a child is confident in using the computer keyboard, stories will flow.

Seymour Papert believes the computer to be a device which allows children: '... to become more like adults, indeed like advanced professionals ...'. A word processor 'can make a child's experience of writing more like that of a real writer' [3].

One device which can greatly facilitate teaching children penmanship is the 'graphics tablet'. It is possible to transcribe from such a tablet onto the computer screen anything which has been drawn, including letters. The parent or teacher can begin by using a transparent overlay with the appropriate letters to be learned. The child then traces with finger, pressure or pen, these letters (or other figures) onto the graphics tablet, which causes the tracings to appear instantly on the screen. The final step involves transferring from screen onto the printer, to take home or to show somebody else. The 'hard copy' is also a way of recording progress.

GRAMMAR AND SYNTAX

'The constant teaching of formal English exercises and grammar indicates that the teacher believes how something is said or written is more important than what is said' [4].

It is very difficult for a teacher to decide when to begin teaching grammatical rules to children. Just as children learn to read and write at their own pace, so it needs a teacher's caring skill to intervene grammatically with a child's reading, writing, and speaking. Too many corrections, too frequently given, can result in a child not wanting to continue reading and writing. We urge all pedants to read Frank Smith's list 'Easy Ways to Make Learning to Read Difficult' [5].

Frank Smith points out that one major difficulty is due to the fact that one word can have many meanings: 'Sock, run, walk, house, fence, bottle, all can be verbs as well as nouns' [6]. This would suggest that it is wise to allow children to write freely and read quite fluently before teaching the rules of grammar. Words spelled incorrectly need correcting, but a page of work produced by a child which is then covered by a teacher's corrective marks can damage a child's confidence and self-esteem. This is not to condone poor spelling; but a careful systematic approach to corrections needs to be thought out.

Using the computer as a word processor is a valuable tool at this stage of the language development. The story is typed out and grammatical or spelling corrections can be made instantly, while the story is still on the screen. If the teacher is not available immediately, the story can be printed out or saved for corrections to be made later. The importance of this method lies in the retention of the original script. The whole story does not need to be rewritten. Its appearance is still neat and professional-looking no matter how many corrections need to be made. When all the corrections have been made the story can be printed as a perfect example of the child's work. Another advantage of the word processor is that more than one copy can be made of the same piece. Dictionary computer programs are an advantage at this level as they can help students to help themselves by allowing spelling checks.

THE THREE Cs

Grammatical rules need to be systematically taught and frequent reminders need to be given. Children very quickly remember what nouns and verbs are, but find difficulty in remembering adjectives and adverbs. These formal rules can be taught most effectively by a proper use of computer programs. By using the computer as a 'fun-tool' for learning these rules, as in 'Word World' and 'Children from Space', the children begin to play at grammar. They no longer find the task arduous or boring. It avoids the damaging effect on morale which a piece of work covered with teacher's corrections can have. The constant fear of being corrected prevents the free flow of creativity and inhibits the rate of assimilating and organizing new information. Yet it is vital that rules and standards of grammar, syntax, and spelling should be learned. Combining a child's creativity with perfect grammar and syntax will best be achieved by the skilled use of carefully graded computer programs. In Chapter 11, we look at the use of LOGO for teaching rules of grammar and further literacy skills. A child's own writing on a word processor, a graphics tablet, or on the screen, using a light pen, can produce a neat and aesthetic piece of work frequently contrasting sharply with the same effort attempted using conventional pen and paper.

PUNCTUATION AND SENTENCE STRUCTURE

On first learning to read, a child is not aware of words as words. This can be seen in the way the writing is produced. The words all run into one another, some of the letters may be reversed, and there may be a mixture of upper and lower case. A youngster has to be taught to separate the words so that everyone can understand the story. At this point the teaching of punctuation and sentence structure is irrelevant. Comprehension, as previously mentioned, is all-important. Later, when a child is writing a sentence, the structure of individual words is not so important. It is what a child is trying to say which is. This does not mean that a teacher should let mistakes pass uncorrected. Gradually, through frequent reading of suitable stories, prose, and poems, by seeing other children's work, and by the attention paid by a teacher, the child begins to realize the

68

importance of punctuation in helping others understand the meaning of the child's story.

Two boys, not noted for their interest in matters academic, had been told about full stops and capital letters on many occasions by various teachers. Now they were writing a story on the computer. Lee had been typing for some time and suddenly stopped. 'It's a long time since we put in a full stop', he said. 'Right', said Andrew, 'we had better put one in now then hadn't we?' Although both boys were academically poor, they were reasonably confident readers. Nevertheless, they had no insight into the importance and rules of punctuation.

```
                The Dragon and The Knight

  Once upon a time there was a Dragon who lived in a cave on a
  hill.  And every  time somone went past the  Dragons cave he
  brove fire over them. And they turend into ashes.   The  King
  sent  a  Knight  out  to  slay  the  Dragon  but non of them
  sucseaded because just before they. Kould slash his cneck he
  sisled them to a crisp but on one Knight the. Dragon ate one
  of them. Dadric was the best. Knight in  town   so   the  King
  sent  for him he whent to the Castle and he had dinner there
  he slept there aswel he met a  princes  the  next  day.   the
  knight had braecfast there but he had to go on his journy on
  his  horse  because it was a long way to the cave but he did
  not.Know that the dragon had went to the kastle and got   the
  princes.  The  knight  herd  the town people shout help help
  dadric said to his horse come on lining to the  kastle.   But
  when the Knight had got there the dragon had tuc the princes
  to its. Kave the knight rode as fast as he could to the kave
  again. He walked into the cave and killed the dragon.


                    By Lee and Andrew
                       Class 9
                      March 1984
```

Once these boys saw their work professionally produced, they began to realize the importance of punctuation. Although their poor presentation did not improve instantly, everybody felt that some sort of breakthrough had been achieved.

THE THREE Cs

What is interesting about Lee and Andrew is that they typify students all over the world who hate writing. Across the Atlantic, Peggy O'Brien, working in New York, has described them as students who scrunched up their writing so as to make it unintelligible [7]. This would, they hoped, disguise their poor spelling, lack of punctuation, and inability to finish even one paragraph of writing in a forty-minute period. Much to Mrs O'Brien's surprise, it was some of these students who were being unusually insistent about having their turn at writing with the computer. Her conclusion: 'Somewhere along the way, these students sensed that this was a machine which could help them redeem their past academic failures .... They see and hold and read (and distribute with unaccustomed pride) the neatly formatted results yielded by the printer at the touch of a button'.

The use of punctuation only comes with continued reading and the practice of writing skills. It is generally accepted that most children have these skills before the age of eleven years. Some children grasp the importance of good presentation of work, which includes correct spellings, punctuation, grammar, and syntax, as soon as they begin writing for others. It is a chore which can be helped enormously by the computer. To quote Seymour Papert: 'For most children rewriting a text is so laborious that the first draft is the final copy and the skill of rereading with a critical eye is never acquired' [8]. Using the word processor children are willing to write more.

An even greater advantage is that children can work either in pairs or in a group to produce a story. This gives rise to a cross-fertilization of ideas. Arguments can take place on how the story will develop. Most stories written in this way can be seen to have a beginning, a middle, and an end. When the teacher corrects the punctuation, grammar, etc., all the children involved in the story benefit as it is 'their story' which is being improved without the laborious rewriting they hate.

One question we need to ask is 'How much longer are children going to need to know how to write?' The use of the computer as a word processor is just the beginning. At the moment, the use of the Qwerty keyboard is becoming increasingly more important.

However, one day it will only be necessary to talk to the computer and our texts will be printed out for us with all our inaccuracies corrected automatically before it is produced. It is our creativity, our imagination, our ingenuity that the computer will be unable to reproduce – at least, for a time to come.

DICTIONARY SKILLS

When a first story is written most children do not know the alphabet and cannot use a dictionary. The first dictionary they encounter is usually a 'word book'. This is given to the child when a teacher knows that a child recognizes most of the letters of the alphabet. Some children come into school having been taught the names of the letters of the alphabet but not the sounds. Once a child attempts to write a story the use of the word book is an important stage of development. A word book is usually designed so that there is a page for every letter of the alphabet. If a child does not know the spelling of a word, the book is taken to the teacher for the word to be written into the word book. It is then transferred by the child into the story. Thus a personalized dictionary is built up containing words that hold interest and meaning for the owner. This word book can be referred to frequently.

Later, children are taught to use very easy dictionaries, usually containing words and pictures to help a youngster to find the word unaided. Gradually the change is made to more and more advanced dictionaries as reading and writing skills develop. Computer programs can help throughout this development, initially helping children to sort out words into alphabetical order. More and more complex words can be quite a challenge. Children enjoy working against each other to see who can sort out very difficult words the quickest. Using a computer in this way is compelling, especially if children can type in the words to test their friends. They delight in finding words which vary as little as possible from each other in their spelling, in order to confound their playmates.

A program, 'Anagrams' allows children to put in a word which

THE THREE Cs

the computer then scrambles at random. Two nine-year-old girls of equal ability, Frances and Andrea, were asked to test each other's spelling. Initially they both typed in words which were as difficult to understand as to spell. This proved to be for them rather a boring exercise. Frances livened it up. She typed in 'mountain' which the program then put into anagram form. While this was happening Andrea had to look away from the screen. Andrea found this quite easy to unscramble after one or two false starts. The next time Frances typed in 'maintain'. Andrea could not believe her luck and typed in 'mountain' which, of course, was incorrect. She had to try again. It took her quite a long time. Next time Frances typed in the word 'resilient' which Andrea found rather difficult to untangle and needed help to spell correctly. Her own words which she typed in were chosen on an ad hoc basis. Frances then chose 'retrieval' as her word. She was becoming much more careful and selective in her choice of words. Andrea realized what was happening and became equally selective. As both girls were equally matched it proved to be a stimulating exercise and encouraged the use of the dictionary more than we have seen previously. Other children in the class varied in their approach. Some emulated Frances, others chose words randomly without any particular pattern emerging from their endeavours.

Coupling the computer to the printed word will be very powerful. One of us is working on a system which includes a printed dictionary which will contain about a thousand of the most common 'simple' words used by children. Several hundred of these words will be encountered in an expanded version of 'Words, Words, Words'. The dictionary will present these words illustrated in the same manner as they appear on the computer screen.

ANTONYMS AND SYNONYMS

Dictionary skills need to be taught separately from writing skills. Too heavy an emphasis on finding the meanings of words while writing creatively can prevent the free flow of ideas. Good computer programs that show exercises of misunderstandings involving the incorrect use of words can be fun and educational. This is important for improving the literary style of students. Initial stories contain simple words and phrases. The study of words and their meanings is important if a student's first attempts are to improve and develop into good, creative, descriptive examples of written English.

Students need to be taught and encouraged to use a Thesaurus. Exercises can be presented using language normally used with certain words underlined. By using a Thesaurus the student can find more poetic or relevant words to enhance the presentation of their work. Similarly, after a student has written a piece of creative work using the word processing facility of a micro, as well as checking with a dictionary, they could be given the opportunity of changing words to make the piece more interesting and appealing to the audience for which it is written.

ABSTRACTING AND COMPREHENDING

From the age of eight years on, most Junior children spend part of their school day working on projects. These can range from a study of the Romans to a study of astronomy, industry, or World War II. Whatever project is undertaken, whether it involves the whole class or a group within the class, the youngsters need to be able to research the subject being studied. There is little value in children copying out pages of information from encyclopaedias, text books or reference books. The group needs to decide by discussion exactly the area to be studied. Each individual within the group can choose to study a different part of the project. At the end the students' findings are put into a cohesive collection of information. Before this can be achieved, students need to spend time discussing both the aims and objectives of the project and how and where the information is to be found and collated. The importance of being able to talk, argue, and agree to work together cannot be over-emphasized. The skill of collecting and collating the information is one which gradually develops. The material selected by the teacher for the children to work from must be at their reading level. From this material the children will need to know how to abstract the relevant information and reject superfluous data. They must learn how to present the information so that they and their peers can understand the work they have carried out.

Data processing using a computer is one of the best ways of using a micro. Information can be stored on disk by a group of children. They will need to decide the headings and how much information can be stored on the disk. From this information quizzes and questionnaires can be formulated to help test the group and other children in the class.

A project on the weather involved the study of wind, rain, temperature, and sunshine. The children were divided into groups. Each group studied and prepared the data on their particular area, e.g. wind – what is wind? what causes gales? where does the wind blow? etc. When preparing their work the children needed to be aware of the fact that the information was to be used by other children and had to be presented at that level. When they had put in all the information on the weather, they then devised questions to test the other children, e.g. what is a prevailing wind? or, what is an area of high pressure?

Another group of children studied the planets. Using FACT-FILE they built up a file of the planets – e.g. where they were in relation to the sun and to the earth. They then devised a series of questions on the planets which other children had to answer: which planet is nearest to the sun? which planet is the oldest?

Both of these projects involved a great deal of research which the children had to undertake themselves (with teacher supervision). The greatest benefit was in having to devise questions. It was easy to see who did or did not understand what they had put into the FACTFILE program.

Much later on, students studying for exams need skill in abstracting information from libraries where row upon row of books hold snippets of valuable information. Many hours are spent by students writing up notes of their findings. With micro technology they should be able to contact libraries, museums, and universities all over the world. The information they receive can then be stored on their own collection of disks.

ADVANCED WRITING USING WORD PROCESSING

In creative writing students need to have wide experience of reading, a stimulating environment, and a sympathetic teacher. When asked to write a story, students will not present a good piece of fiction if it is going to be severely criticized by a teacher. A word processor allows the students the opportunity of correcting their own work before presenting it to the teacher as a finished product. A sympathetic teacher can help them correct their work as they write. Altering phraseology, changing paragraphs, correcting spelling can all be done on the first draft. A student writes for the teacher as an audience. The audience should show positive response and not negative. A stimulating environment can be created in the classroom. However, students often tend to write of their experiences outside the classroom – about their homes, the town, or television or video programmes – all affect the way students write their stories. They present lurid accounts of murders or kidnappings as if they were everyday occurrences in their lives. Teachers need to counteract this influence by giving students wide fictional reading facilities and allowing their students to express their feelings, fears, and frustrations without belittling their efforts. A word processor helps these efforts; as it is printed, the student's work looks professional in its presentation.

In addition, programs are appearing which help pupils to start writing stories by providing a choice of animated sequences. Story starter and story maker type programs teach children to think of what happened? to whom? where? when? what were they doing? Or, (1) A person, animal, character was (2) doing something (3) in, on, under, somewhere. The use of clever, animated graphics stimulates children's imagination and provides a sense of structure. Other programs encourage students to think of stories in terms of a beginning, a middle, and an end.

THE THREE Cs

SHAKESPEARE, *et al.*

Think of the improvements in studying Shakespeare when the plays are available on interactive videodisks. Not only will the drama come to life, the commentary will provide clues to the more obscure passages, perhaps presenting parts of it in a contemporary idiom. By comparing and contrasting two presentations – one in the classic tradition, one in the modern vernacular – a whole new insight may be gained. A study of Shakespeare may be extended to cover other areas such as music, history, and geography. For example, the large number of musical compositions which are based on Shakespeare, from Berlioz's 'Romeo and Juliet', and Mendelssohn's 'Midsummer Night's Dream', right up to Bernstein's 'West Side Story', would serve as a nice introduction to programme music. Videodisks should also allow historical and geographical trips related to Tudor times and places.

Adventure games, the latest craze in computer games, use interactive videodisks. Write your own ending to *Hamlet* or *Macbeth*! We know of one program being developed (not yet involving videodisks) based on St John the Divine's *Revelation*. Fight the forces of evil on Doomsday! This may raise the hackles of some. But that's missing the point: the potential for putting life and drama into some of the old tales and classic literature is enormous.

Historical adventure games and simulations such as 'The Charge of the Light Brigade', 'Mary Rose', 'Saqquara' [9], and Australia's 'The First Ships', are excellent examples of the shape of things to come. Good education should be entertaining. These programs surely both educate and entertain.

Spinnaker's 'Snooper Troops' (aimed at older children and adults) is an adventure game of a very different ilk. You are the detective who has to solve a crime. Somebody stole the performing dolphin from the local aquarium. Without going into the details of this fascinating game, the act of becoming an effective detective is the best education for becoming a scientist we know of. You uncover clues, interview suspects, and solve the crime only by being logical and precise, maintaining meticulous notes, and persevering for many hours.

Chapter 7
Communication and Life Skills

CORRESPONDING VIA ELECTRONIC MAIL

When children first learn to write they delight in writing letters to friends, relatives, or pen pals. Normally, this enthusiasm gradually wanes until, in the end, it becomes a chore. Teachers need to help children to write to each other, to become pen pals. Letters are also written to holiday resorts, industrial concerns, and Father Christmas. Usually these letters are 'one-off' and do not consist of prolonged correspondence. Writing to pen pals may be encouraged by parents or teachers, but the association does not last very long. Two or three letters, perhaps, and then interest fades. Obviously, there are exceptions: some children, as they grow into their teens, travel abroad to stay with their pen pals.

In our experience, using the pen pal system on the computer was much more successful. The system built up gradually at Norton Glebe Primary School, with a few girls corresponding with a group at another school. As the school year progressed, more of the class joined in the project and exchanged letters. We found out about the others' school, uniforms, football results, hobbies, etc. We sent birthday cards and a computerized card for Christmas.

This, we hope, is only the beginning. Children can begin as early as five years to use a computer as a word processor. They can type sentences and illustrate them on the print-out sheets. Gradually, the stories get longer and more involved. This does not need to be a solitary exercise. Two or more children can be involved. Once the PRESTEL system becomes cheap enough and widespread enough, we would expect a large number of schools to use this valuable facility to aid young children to write to each other.

Pupils are often encouraged to write to students in other countries, notably France. Again it can become a chore as the main intention is to improve the writing of French. With an English/French dictionary database to aid translation it could be much more fun — therefore sustained for longer periods.

When working on projects in school, letters are written to various agencies asking for information. Waiting for replies can take months. If there is a reply, it often comes back at a time when the interest and enthusiasm for the project has completely disappeared. All the teacher can do is set it aside for use some time in the future with another class.

The computer will eventually supersede these sources and become a prime source of information. Requests for information can be answered immediately. In April 1985, the Time Network for Schools came into operation. This is an Electronic Central Database which schools are able to consult and make contributions to. It contains a variety of information relating to both curricular and extra-curricular activities. Career and job vacancies can also be shown to older students who will be able to apply through the system. Administration, information, individual messages, and software can all be entered into the data bases. It is hoped to expand the system internationally.

Not unrelated, in 1984, the UK's Manpower Services Commission created an electronic bulletin board. The system allowed users to link 'notice boards' on which to post information about MSC programmes and projects which involve the use of new technology, computer-based training, interactive video, authoring languages and systems, teleconferencing, etc. The system also offered an electronic mail service, allowing registered users to post their own private and public messages, questions, etc. to specific individuals on all users. Ultimately, such a system should be expanded to serve as a gigantic clearing house for all sorts of job, training, and career information, as well as for posting vacancies and employment opportunities.

Gradually, as more and more libraries and museums feed their collections into computers, we are going to have more and more knowledge – literally at our finger tips. It will be possible to request information from another town in another country and to receive the answer printed out on our computers either at home or at school. A school in Wales working on a project on oil should be able to receive information from Aberdeen about the oil rigs in the North Sea, from Texas on land-based oil wells, from Calgary where oil needs to be extracted by two different methods, etc. Collecting this kind of information conventionally could take months. Collected via electronic mail, such information could be printed out for dissemination within a day or a week.

Another advantage is that the computer can produce graphs and simulations in a way much more exciting to the pupils. If students are to keep pace with the massive growth in information technology, schools, colleges, and homes need to be linked to world-wide sources of information.

Children will still be able to pass notes to each other in class, perhaps through the microwriter, or on a grubby piece of paper sneaked under the table. The choice should be theirs. Application forms for university or employment could be stored in a data file so that sending off form after identical form, expending a lot of time and money, could end. Information and the world of communication will be in our homes, in our schools, and in the offices. It will be the task of the educators to decide how to take advantage of this bank of knowledge.

CYCLOPS

CYCLOPS is a telewriting system developed at the Open University for distance tutoring. It transmits not only the customary typewriting, but also handwriting and diagrams, down an ordinary telephone line. The tutor, sitting at a CYCLOPS terminal, can communicate with students in up to ten different centres. The tutor can communiate by voice, or through drawings created by moving a light-pen over CYCLOPS screen. Alternatively, the tutor may use an electronic 'scribble pad' to transmit more complex diagrams. This can be done by placing the prepared diagram on the flat surface of the pad, and then tracing over it with a special ball-pen connected by a wire to the CYCLOPS terminal. At any point during the tutorial, the tutor may replace a prepared tape. An ordinary audio-cassette tape holds both graphics and, if needed, synchronized sound. Once the tutor has placed a picture on the students' screens, any one of them may alter or add to it.

Telewriting offers new kinds of distance communication. Mathematical formulae, maps, and other diagrams which may be almost impossible to describe in words, can be easily communicated simply by drawing them on a screen.

As Mike Sharples, reviewing this system, has pointed out: 'Spoken words fade as soon as they are uttered, so talk is a series of individual acts: one person makes a statement or asks a question, another replies. Pictures, or written words, linger until they are deliberately erased, so a telewriting conversation can build up a shared image: students at CYCLOPS tutorials often work together to create a single list or diagram. Any medium has a structure that affects the quality of communication, and telewriting seems to encourage co-operation rather than confrontation' [1].

FACTFILE

CYCLOPS was designed for Open University students. It presupposes certain kinds of communication skills. FACTFILE is a simple program which was designed as a result of a seminar at the University of Cambridge Department of Education in 1981. Teachers and children in primary school, it was felt, needed a gentle introduction to the storage and retrieval of data in a microcomputer which did not require the coded commands of the sophisticated information retrieval systems such as CYCLOPS and PRESTEL. The function of the program is to introduce the children to the basic principles needed for creating their own data base. The program allows the children to build up their own files of data on any topic which they choose.

The program begins by welcoming the child to FACTFILE. Then provides a choice as follows:

You can
  A   Make a file
  B   Change a file
  C   Look at the file
  D   Start again
Press A B C or D.

The children would presumably press A and the computer would then come back with

Make a file
What is your file called?
Type it then press RETURN

Suppose the children decide on shapes; then a few frames later the computer may ask them, 'How many headings do you have under shapes?' And it goes on in this way. This provides some of the basic skills necessary, first for creating, then for searching through, data bases. These must be considered as among the most important skills children can learn. It is one thing to write things down in a notebook – certainly children can extend their memory by having things written down in their own word book. But in the long run, as we shall see later (Chapter 11), children will need to grow up knowing how to use 'expert systems'. No notebook will rearrange information for them. No notebook can do anything other than simply recall information put into it. Computer data bases, on the other hand, can establish relationships which may not be obvious at the time of note-taking. Therefore, this must become one of the basic skills children learn – skills which will be necessary in the future in order to communicate effectively.

COMPUTER-BASED TRAINING

We define the term 'training' here as providing information with a view to achieving a particular job skill. Such training may be

81

exceedingly limited, if it involves low grade skills. It may also be extensive, taking many years, as in the case of training a medical doctor. Training should not be confused with education, which has a much broader objective. Education aims not only at achieving a satisfactory job skill but also at achieving an understanding of the world. In addition, education involves developing the individual to his or her maximum personal potential.

Among the most powerful of computer-based training systems are those involving simulations. An airline pilot is not put simply into a 747 to fly it on the job. A potential 747 pilot is going to spend many hours in a cockpit simulating the controls and having in front of him a screen or a series of screens controlled by computers which give him the visual effects of actually flying the aircraft. Simulating flight on a computer screen has been transferred in a more limited version to microcomputers.

Simulating flight on a home microcomputer makes it into a game: 'You are in charge — you fly the airplane'. Such simulation software will proliferate over the next decades, allowing children to pretend that they are astronauts, train drivers, supertanker captains, bridge builders, town planners, highway engineers, factory managers, doctors, nurses, etc. The educational value of these games should be self-evident.

At the professional level, one does not want airline pilots to be trained on very expensive equipment such as a super jet airliner. The same is true for doctors working with patients. Unfortunately, much medical training is still on-the-job training at great expense to the patients going through the medical mills of our time. We will describe in greater detail the use of computers in medicine and in medical training in Chapter 11. Suffice it to say that when medical expert systems become widespread, both diagnosis and treatment for the average patient will improve greatly.

Not only the training of physicians, but also the training of psychiatrists can be helped by simulations. There exists a program called 'Parry' created by Professor Colby, which simulates a paranoiac. It is reminiscent of the earlier programs, produced by Professor Joseph Weizenbaum at MIT, known as 'Eliza' [2]. A computer can be made to simulate personalities. This property allows the creation of programs for training potential salesmen and, for that matter, all forms of people-to-people jobs in which tact and diplomacy are needed.

The possibility of interacting with computers which simulate various personalities in various group situations will be of great value for accelerating the development of social skills. One would be less than human to set oneself up to be humiliated − to make a fool of oneself in front of others. But people generally don't mind doing just that with a computer. At least not in private. We will look at the use of simulation for increasing sensitivity and social skills, as well as the use of computers for psychological testing, a little later on in this chapter.

ADVANCED HARDWARE AND SOFTWARE SYSTEMS

It may be appropriate at this point just to reiterate the power of the technology as it is shaping up. Bruce Lang Associates of the UK and Belgium specialize in producing computer-based training packages [3]. The hardware consists of a mix of the following systems. An ordinary computer, the IBM PC, is coupled to an interactive video system produced by Philips. To this is added a telex terminal. The system allows diagrams, slides, cartoons, i.e. pictures of any sort, to be projected onto the screen from the video system. Superimposed on the visuals, can be text introduced by the telex component. That means any headings, labels, or questions can be placed anywhere on the screen superimposed on the picture. One other important feature: a device is placed around the edge of the screen which uses infra-red light with sensors at the opposite sides, such that if a finger touches the screen it interrupts these very thin beams of infra-red light. The computer detects exactly where on the screen the finger is pointing.

This system allows one to eliminate the keyboard altogether. For example, the system has been adapted for training automobile mechanics. Pictures of various engine components appear on the screen. Questions appear at the bottom of the screen and the trainee is asked to point to various portions of the screen in response to the questions. Note how the trainee does not have to use a keyboard in working with this interactive system. All he or she needs to do is point to the appropriate place on the screen. This system does not just allow the trainee to point to a particular component of the picture, the screen may act as a sheet of paper asking multiple choice questions for the trainee to answer by pointing to A B C D E, or whatever answer the question requires. Such systems are not only useful for training mechanics for automobiles or aeroplanes; one can also immediately see their use in medicine, in biology, in geography, etc.

The National Railways in Holland have used a similar system for instructing their train drivers in emergency procedures [4]. At the moment these systems still cost as much as a medium-priced automobile. However, it is reasonable to believe that ten years from now they will have dropped by a factor of ten, if not more. Certainly, cheaper systems are already available using light pens or, for example, the 'mouse' used by the Apple Macintosh. The mouse sits on the desk or table, attached by a cord to the computer. By moving it around on the table, one can move the cursor around on the screen. When the cursor is in the desired position, pressing the button on the mouse, enters the information into the computer. The mouse can therefore be used as a pointing finger. It is also a marvellous device for drawing. All these systems will be further strengthened when cheap voice chips and voice-to-print devices become available. The trainee, whether doctor or mechanic, will merely talk to the computer or point to the screen as indicated above.

COMPUTER AND CAREER CHOICES

At the moment, the transition from school or university to work is very badly organized. Students are frequently turfed out into the world with very little helpful information. In many instances career advice is left to teachers who are neither trained for the job nor paid for it. The situation is still largely unsatisfactory.

Even going to university, which is a momentous decision, is often

Plate 1A. Hardware. The computer itself, including the keyboard, can be seen in front. At the back, on the left, is a tape recorder which acts as the input device for the computer. Back right is the VDU, or CRT, whose television screen allows the computer to express the output. The reader is referred to the Glossary (Appendix D) for further explanations of these terms. (Ken Price, Phototronics)

Plate 1B. Software. The picture shows a collection of tapes and floppy disks on which are stored the various learning programs, some of which are described in this book. (Ken Price, Phototronics)

Plate 2. Two boys playing 'Hangman', one of the more popular spelling games. (Ken Price, Phototronics)

Plate 3. Video games are popular the world over. Here boys in Shanghai are busily engaged playing such a game. (Tom Stonier)

Plate 4A. Abacus. The abacus is an ancient Chinese device used for doing lengthy sums and calculations. When it comes to doing sums, an adroit user of the abacus can actually outpace a less adroit user on a pocket calculator. (Tom Stonier)

Plate 4B. Log tables and slide rule. Before the advent of computers complex calculations in science and engineering were performed using log tables and slide rules. (Tom Stonier)

Plate 5. Cathy Conlin and some of her pupils working on a computer. (Ken Price, Phototronics)

Plate 6. Two girls working with the 'Let's Count' program. Although this is a mathematics program, the visual images such as a ship and islands allows for classroom discussion about ships, finding islands, and what it's like to live on an island.
(Ken Price, Phototronics)

Plate 7. Two boys working on a word processor.
(Ken Price, Phototronics)

(Ken Price, Phototronics)

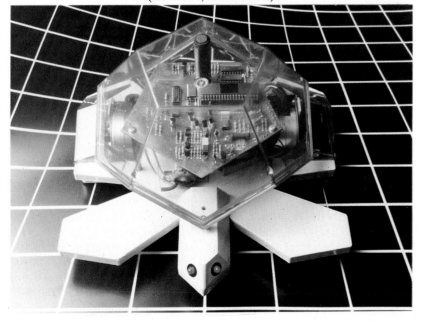

Plate 8. Children working with a remote-controlled robot turtle as part of learning LOGO and other subjects. (Supplied by Valiant Designs, London)

Plate 9. The Elm system. The Elm system allows a teacher to produce his own software with great ease. Pupils enjoy working with programs that they feel have been designed especially for them by their teacher. (Tom Stonier)

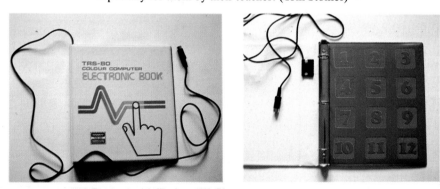

Plates 10A & 10B. A Computer book. The upper plate shows the TRS-80 Colour Computer Electronic Book. The lower plate shows the inside of the book with the concept keyboard of twelve switches in the back. It is possible to overlay many pages on this concept keyboard which could have twelve individual questions or answers, or some other written material. More dramatic is an actual picture. For example, a traffic scene with a traffic light over switch 5: if the child presses down on the traffic light, it activates switch 5 and the graphics on the computer screen now cause the light to change from red to green. The full potential of these books has not yet been recognized by the profession.
(Supplied by Crystal Presentations, Birmingham)

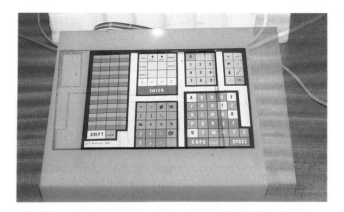

Plate 11. Concept keyboard. A large concept keyboard designed by one of the authors to get away from the traditional Qwerty keyboard. The letters, numbers, punctuations, and other functions are arranged in a logical fashion, easy to remember and easy to find. The colour coding is a further aid for the young child just learning the rigours of the English alphabet. There are actually 176 positions possible on this keyboard including (in the green area) a large number of special function keys. The keyboard is designed for one-finger typists using the right hand for letters and the left hand for other functions. A left handed version is equally possible. (Tom Stonier)

Plate 12. Graphics tablet. Teacher using a graphics tablet tracing out a simple face onto the screen. Graphics tablets can be used not only for a variety of artistic and design problems, but for the simple act of teaching letters and words. (Tom Stonier)

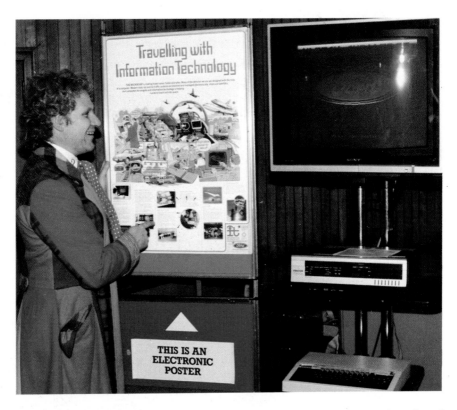

Plate 13. Electronic display board. Or the 'electronic poster' is an enlarged version of the 'computer book' (Plate 10). Pressing areas on the poster, causes things to happen on the screen. (Supplied by Crystal Presentations, Birmingham)

left to chance. At a time when a pupil ought to have maximum information, because once he or she is in the system it is very difficult to shift, the amount of information, and the nature of the information, is frequently purely a hit-and-miss proposition. It is gratifying to note, therefore, that in Britain the Educational Counselling and Credit Transfer Information Service based at Milton Keynes put itself on to the PRESTEL GATEWAY system in 1984. Potential candidates are able to dial a local telephone number and key straight into the Open University computer to search for information on courses directly. The ECCTIS has had sixteen thousand personal enquiries in 1984, mostly about the first degree and full-time course sector. However, enquiries about part-time courses are about a third of those for full-time courses. The computer system initially had twenty-one thousand courses on file and was beginning to build up the non-advanced courses [5].

The above represents what might be considered the administration of education in the life of an individual. But there is a much more sophisticated use of computers which has been worked up by Dr Roger Lucas, formerly of the Southern General Hospital in Glasgow. Dr Lucas is the psychologist and director of Insight Centres, based in Glasgow. Insight Centres have developed a series of computer-based tests to help a person to choose a career. The following is abstracted from a brochure put out by Insight Centres [6]:

When you apply for a job or a place on a course, a good interviewer will attempt to obtain a balanced view of seven or eight aspects of your application. You may think that all he looks for is just your qualifications, your experience, and your 'character'. The first two are cut and dried facts − hard data. You have them or you don't. You know them and you tell them. However, a good interviewer looks for other aspects. For example, special aptitudes which you may possess: skills with figures, with words, with abstract ideas, skills with your hands, aptitude for mechanical things or, very important, the skill of knowing how to get along with other people. The interviewer will also look for interests, not just keenness or alertness, but a general pattern of your interests. Are you practical, an organiser, a helper, is your inclination towards science or the arts? Things are obviously done better by people with a strong personal involvement.

Thirdly, he looks for signs that your personal disposition matches a list of personality factors or temperaments which he feels are important for carrying out the job well and with personal satisfaction. Finally, he checks out your health, physical characteristics such as strength, or voice, or whatever other factors may be important to the job. An experienced interviewer knows that the process is not quite as tidy and systematic as it looks on paper. Often the interviewer's specifications are incomplete. But that is the general framework in which the interviewer works. The computer is able, by and large, to ask the same kinds of questions a personnel officer can. It can also evaluate the verbal answer. What the computer cannot do is, of course, study your features and, in particular, the body language, the facial expressions − the non-verbal communication systems which are so important. Nevertheless, the standard aptitude tests devised by psychologists over many years − in spite of their limitations, can be of some help to an experienced personnel officer. And these aptitude tests can be administered by a computer.

The way the computer is used is simple. You sit comfortably in front of the computer which will display various questions and diagrams. You answer the questions by pressing the appropriate buttons on a small concept keyboard with very few specific choices. They may be limited to YES, NO, OCCASIONALLY, DON'T KNOW, DON'T UNDERSTAND, PASS. The computer digests the responses and then puts up the next question. Unlike a written test where the next question appears irrespective of the answer you gave on the previous question, a computer will adjust its set of questions to your responses.

The first test concentrates on taking an inventory of your interests. It is later fed back to you to show how your pattern compares with those of a wide range of occupations. There are no right or wrong answers, and you proceed at your own pace. Most people will take an hour to work through it.

The next inventory is a mixture of likes and dislikes which can be analysed to show how you compare with other people. Finally, you get a chance to complete a test of aptitudes which are of general importance in guiding you as to what type of occupation you would be most suited for. These responses are timed and the whole process takes about two and a half hours. At the end the computer prints out an INSIGHT profile, an individually compiled document which tells you in clear, simple language with helpful graphics, how you have scored and what it means in broad terms. This is presented by the resident counsellor who will invite you to read it and discuss it.

Some years ago, one of us (TS) had occasion to try out this INSIGHT program. I was not really interested in spending an hour or two on it, but was interested in the sorts of questions that came up. I therefore resolved to answer questions with very little thought, and if it did require thought, to simply push buttons at random. When it came to the mathematical aptitude part, the questions were all multiple choice. My first thought was to answer them at random where it involved any difficulty. However, I decided to use my pocket calculator instead and run through the maths section using my pocket calculator.

When the computer had finished compiling all my answers in all the sections and printed it out, I was rather eager to examine its response *vis-à-vis* my mathematical powers. The computer stated bluntly:

THE SPEED AND ACCURACY OF YOUR RESPONSE IMPLIES THAT YOU WERE USING AN ELECTRONIC CALCULATOR.

I was both shocked and delighted.

Of course, a good program testing for aptitudes must look at the speed of a response as well as its accuracy, and the computer had been programmed to do that. It had even, as I discovered, been programmed to take into account the possibility that a person, like me, would resort to a pocket calculator rather than work it out in my head or with a pencil and a piece of paper.

For companies wishing to use the system for interviewing prospective candidates, they may use the Centre for testing or, alternatively, the system is sufficiently portable that it can be carried out at the client's organizations' own premises. Each applicant individually, one at a time can work on his or her own, in complete privacy. Coffee or assistance are available at the touch of a special button.

Three things make this service an important milestone. First, it allows a wide variety of standardized psychological tests to be administered using a computer. This removes the classroom aura of paper and pencil administration and restores the proper dignity, involvement, and privacy to the process. Secondly, these sets of computer programs produce interpretations of the test results in plain, readable English within a few minutes of testing. Once the results have been absorbed, the person has the opportunity of discussing his report with an experienced consultant. The feedback is virtually immediate. Third, because of computerization, advances in the tests themselves are being developed. The information gained in the first answers a person gives are used as a basis for choosing subsequent questions to ask, so that reliable measurements (as reliable as these kinds of tests are) can be achieved with only a quarter or a third of the usual number of questions.

The tests used by the Insight Centres are extremely helpful in providing personnel officers with clues to potential candidates. They can also be very helpful to a candidate in assessing his or her own strengths and weaknesses. These tests are designed primarily with a view to filling jobs or selecting careers. However, they could be used, if properly extended, as a sort of personality mirror. Such a personality mirror would apply to many other life situations such as retirement choices, choices of life decisions, and in the last analysis, even how to face death. A pioneer of such studies, Dr Mildred Shaw, formerly with the Centre for the Study of Human Learning at Brunel University, has pointed out that computers lend themselves superbly well to a content-free dialogue with people. The virtually instant processing of people's responses, coupled to the neutral replies, helps people '. . . to become more aware of the patterns of thought and feeling implicit in their responses' [7].

If some adults may feel uncomfortable about consulting a computer, children generally don't. Doctor Mary Humphrey of Palo Alto, California, reports that some children would be only too happy to have the computer as a 'friend'. For example, ten-year-old Jeff commented that he would like to '. . . have it talk with me and solve personal problems'. Eleven-year-old Satomi said, 'I would like to talk with it and discuss my problems so the computer can give its opinion' [8].

Work being conducted at the University of Hull includes creating a psychology data base. These data bases will be the forerunners of expert systems coupled to the sorts of aptitude tests described above for the INSIGHT program. When they do, it will become increasingly possible for individuals to discover their own psychological profiles. In a few instances, it may become very clear that there are certain pathological aspects.

One of the most obvious pathological manifestations of a mix of social, physiological, and psychological problems, is alcoholism. Two of our students, Julie Davey and Andy Chudzik, devised a computerized questionnaire to aid in the diagnosis of alcoholism. The project was carried out in conjunction with an alcoholism unit at a local hospital and was well received. Many of the factors discussed above emerged in this project. The advantages of a computer program which would respond to the nature of the answer, became apparent early on. The written questionnaire was cumbersome. It involved some two hundred questions. Irrespective of the answer given to question 17, question 18 would not change its wording. In contrast, the computer could move on to question 38 rather than to question 18, in accordance with the response to question 17. The novelty and the privacy encouraged patients to stay with the program and there was reason to believe that the patients were, as in the Glasgow situation, more honest in answering the questions from the computer. The program not only asked questions, but provided information: for example, the annual financial cost to the patient of imbibing daily large quantities of liquor.

In the long run, these programs are designed to find their way into the privacy of all homes. This can be done either by selling separate software or, more likely, by having it incorporated into a PRESTEL-type system so that the individual may access it through his or her own television/telephone system.

SIMULATIONS TO INCREASE AWARENESS AND SENSITIVITY

The above programs would be largely diagnostic. Their function would be to make a person more aware of his own strengths and weaknesses, his potential assets, and his potential problem areas. The computer can provide more than that, however. Not only may it provide information, e.g. through expert systems in psychology, or useful information with respect to specific problems such as alcoholism, venereal disease, or other psychological or physical problems, but it will also be able to provide another dimension. This dimension is perhaps achieved best by means of simulations.

THE THREE Cs

One of our postgraduate students, Colin Price, who is a religious education teacher, has developed a 'boy meets girl' program [9]. Although the computer will never substitute for a girl, or for a boy, it does allow an awkward teenager to start thinking out what might be the responses given by different types of personalities in different types of situations. The program has been most successful in stimulating classroom discussions and personal thoughts. In principle, programs of this sort can be extended to situations such as:

Baby sitter meets parents
Baby sitter meets child
How to handle parents (for children)
How to handle children (for parents)
Nurse meets patient
Doctor meets patient

Simulations could relate to family interactions, relations with grandparents, relations between husbands and wives, etc. Simulations can also be enormously helpful in potential bargaining situations. These would include interviews with:

Prospective employers
Social workers
Doctors
Bureaucrats
Bank managers
Travel agents
University or polytechnic admission officers

Such programs would represent simulations of potential confrontations. They would involve situations of group, or individual, conflict and could be useful in teaching about labour-management bargaining techniques, or business negotiations. The ability to simulate group dynamics with respect to conflict and cooperation should be of interest also to international negotiators trying to work out a treaty between countries. Such simulations should become standard in developing the new field of peace studies.

Lastly, simulations are also an extremely good way of learning how to handle potential emergencies. On microcomputer now there are programs about what to do in case of an oil spill: BP's SLICK deals with such a situation. There are programs on nuclear reactors, there are other programs under development dealing with other kinds of emergencies.

CONCLUDING REMARKS

We will expand further on the above discussion, particularly in Chapter 11. What should be clear by now is that experts are creating simulations which will relate more and more to real-life situations. The computer will be used not merely to help children how to read and write, but also at advanced levels to train automotive mechanics, advanced engineers, doctors, and other professionals. Further, computer-based education will not be limited to job-related, computer-based training (CBT), but will expand to encompass a wide range of life skills − from understanding better the great literature, to understanding how to get along better with other people.

Section III
Advice for teachers, parents, and academics

Chapter 8
Classroom Dynamics (for Teachers only)

When pocket calculators were first introduced into comprehensive schools there was a great deal of opposition. The uninformed believed that they would encourage students to be lazy and prevent the teaching/learning of basic mathematics. What has actually happened is that the students are now expected to use their calculators to work through problems of a much more complex nature. Today, students are not able to complete advanced examinations without calculators.

With help from the UK's Department of Industry virtually every school in Great Britain now has access to computers. Initially, integrating computers into schools caused problems. Reactions varied from suppressed concern to overt hostility. In secondary schools it was firmly believed, especially by maths teachers that computers were destined for the maths department. It took a while to realize that micros cut across curriculum boundaries and were not the sole province of mathematics.

In primary schools the problems were different. Headteachers had to decide which class or group of children were to use the computer. Some simply placed it in the class of the oldest children and there it remained for all time. Others decided to allow only the 7–11-year-old children to use the computer. It was placed on a trolley and trundled from one class to another. Still others set up a computer room and children were sent to the room when it was their turn. The biggest headaches were reserved for headteachers of large schools: the Department of Industry offered only one micro to each school, irrespective of whether there were three classes or twenty-two.

THE THREE Cs

Some headteachers were not interested in microtechnology at all. They simply passed the responsibility of the computer to a member of staff. If the school had a computer-orientated teacher, both staff and children were fortunate indeed. Such teachers viewed the introduction of the computer as an opportunity rather than as a problem. The teacher had to find ways of integrating the micro into the life of the class. There were several ways of achieving this, depending on the age of the children, the software available, and the aims and objectives to be attained. Almost always, the computer (providing it was not left to moulder in some closet) became a centre of attention and excitement in the classroom.

HOW MANY CHILDREN ON A COMPUTER?

This can vary according to how the computer is being used. If a program is being used with very young children, it is better to have only two children sitting at the computer. Obviously other children will wander over and stay a while. However, only two should be designated as working through the program. The way they work together can be fascinating to observe. Great insight into how they think and understand their environment can be gained by a teacher listening and watching the behaviour of the children using a micro. No other educational tool encourages as much productive conversation. Very young children using Michael Holt's early maths program, 'Let's Count', considered the possibility of living on an island. They discussed the need to find food, drink, and somewhere to live. The music of the 'Drunken Sailor' (which is incorporated into the program) encouraged the children to sing the chorus.

Drill and practice programs usually do not favour much discussion; their educational value is minimal. However, less able children may gain a sense of security and success when allowed to work through such programs. Letters and numbers always appear the right way round, and also in a left to right sequence − in contrast to their own writing and maths books. It is easier for them to press the keys than to form the letters. The delete button is of value to all children: mistakes no longer cause embarrassment. Problem solving and simulation programs e.g. 'Mary Rose' and 'Slick' can involve a group of older children learning to work together. They can argue intensely without causing any serious break-ups of relationships. The computer in this situation acts as the referee. Each team or group discusses the problem and possible ways of solving it. The computer has what is accepted as the correct answer, thereby preventing further arguments.

'Grannie's Garden' has been worked through by groups of younger children including an entire class. Although it quickly became boring to older children, it did provide interesting reading material for younger, and slow readers. For them, repetition was enjoyable as they learned to master the material. 'Great Britain' involved a whole class working on a computer project which did not revolve solely around the computer. In this program the children had to become involved in a General Election. They had to design posters and slogans, give election addresses, and create a manifesto. One Party who thought they could win by abolishing income tax received a sharp rebuff from the program.

PEER TEACHING

One of the most successful ways of integrating the micro into the classroom is to use the monitorial system. Using a program with which you are familiar, choose two of your more able children. Provide the remainder of the class with activities which require minimum supervision from you. This need not take too much time. Explain to the two children how the program works and work through it with them until they understand what is required of them. Leave them to work through it on their own. Return to your normal method of teaching, only going to the two at the computer in the normal course of your movements around the class. When they have finished, allow one child to remain at the computer and choose another child so they work through the program together. The first child teaches the newcomer. Repeat this process as often as needed until all the children who are able have become familiar with the program. This repetition of working through a program is not, as might at first be thought, a waste of time. In a class of mixed ability the interaction between the two children is worth noting. The child who is acting as the teacher is able to act in a dominant role. This is beneficial in a variety of ways. First, a child with leadership qualities can use these qualities to help others. Second, a more able child can help a child with learning difficulties. Third, a shy child who has been given the task of teaching another child will talk and take charge without hesitation. Children who have difficulty forming figures and letters are very happy to take control of the keyboard when teaching the program to a peer. The bossy child in the class has something constructive to offer where there is no place for aggression.

When two children sit in front of a computer one almost always plays the dominant role. The dominant child sits on the edge of the seat, fingers hovering over the keyboard. The chair is moved so that it is immediately in front of the computer even though the teacher had carefully placed the two chairs equidistant from the micro. In other words, the dominant one takes charge. When assigning children to monitorial roles according to the system described above, any child in the class can be the dominant one. On one occasion two children of equal ability were asked to work on the program. They solved the problem without even speaking. One happily took charge of the keyboard. The other equally happily decided on the answers and in reality did most of the brain work.

THE IMPORTANCE OF TALK AND SOCIALIZING

In 1870 the Education Act of that year adopted five as the lower age limit for compulsory attendance at school. It was not until the Education Act of 1944 that schools were separated into primary, secondary, and further education. Since that time many changes have taken place in education. Among the most important has been the change in educational emphasis from the subject taught to the way children learn. We now know that unless children speak we cannot know what they are thinking, nor whether they have understood what they are learning. Even after the 1944 Education

Act children were still expected to sit in silence at school and to work without speaking. Unnecessary speech was severely dealt with by the teachers. The only time children were allowed to speak was when they were chanting their tables or engaged in other rote learning undertaken by the whole class, or when reading to their teacher.

With the development of individual or group learning, the importance of speech became recognized. It is now understood that children need to ask questions of their peers and adults. They need to exchange ideas to verbally test theories. Children who do not have a large spoken vocabulary generally have difficulty in learning to read. Therefore the onus is on the teacher to provide a stimulating environment which will promote speech, argument, and discussion. As previously stated, no other educational tool encourages conversation as much as does the computer. Even the quietest child in the class loses any inhibition when working through a program. It is of course important that the children do not work on their own. During the course of some research we placed a tape recorder with an inbuilt microphone next to the computer. The conversation was stimulating and to the point. With children of primary school age the length of time they can concentrate on any particular piece of work is not very long. On the other hand, children using a micro will go to extraordinary lengths to prolong their stay at the computer.

Normally teachers are careful and naturally keep an eye on children working on the computer. However, it can be interesting and informative to watch children working without teacher interference. One such occasion involved two girls using a program called 'Tuckshop'. This involved buying sweets, crisps, or ice-cream at varied prices. The children started off with 19p. The two girls had bought several items and were left with 2p. This meant they could buy a toffee bar for 2p, or two blackjacks at 1p each. Instead, both girls insisted on asking for crisps or ice-cream. The computer insisted several times that they did not have enough money, but still they persisted. At 2.15 pm the bell rang for playtime. Immediately one girl turned to the other and said, 'Right, it's time to go, let's buy the bar of toffee'. This they did, finished the program, and went out to play. On another occasion two boys using the same program, bought nineteen blackjacks, one at a time. Obviously, this allowed them to stay on the computer longer than if they had bought the more expensive items.

The difficulty facing a teacher is being vigilant enough to give everyone a fair share of time. Naturally, if it is a problem-solving program involving group work, such difficulties do not arise. The entire class becomes involved in discussion and the use of the computer. The skill of the teacher is needed for making up the teams. In teams of mixed ability it is important that the less able gain from the experience. Often the less able are the very children who can use the keyboard to feed the decision taken by the group into the computer. This builds up their confidence, placing them on more equal terms with their peers. If the two groups are of equal ability, it can be exciting to see the depth of understanding and the lengths the children will go to to achieve victory.

THE IMPORTANCE OF PRIVACY

It may seem a paradox, after stating the benefits of using the micro with more than one child, that attention should be drawn to the need for privacy in learning. Nevertheless, one of the most important uses of micros with children is the privacy which the computer affords them. They can make mistakes without the teacher seeing them. One of the first buttons a child learns to press is the delete button. All programs have built-in rewards or corrections, so intervention by the teachers in the learning process is seldom necessary. The role of the teacher is in the care taken to choose the program as a suitable match for the children's need and capability. Built into the program can be checks and results for the teacher to call up when the program is finished. While the children are working through the program it is beneficial to leave them to work on their own. This builds up their confidence as they feel in control of their own learning. When they press the delete button the mistake is tidily erased so that, at the end, the teacher is confronted with a finished piece of work, neatly presented.

Privacy is doubly important to slow learners of all ages – not only *vis-à-vis* the teacher, but also *vis-à-vis* their peers. At home they may also feel embarrassed towards their parents or siblings. Slow learners of older age benefit even more. When they use computers, they feel they are using advanced technology or, depending on their previous experience, an amusement arcade toy. The fact that they are actually learning a basic skill (e.g. reading) is not always of interest to them. In remedial classes, individual teenagers using language and maths programs will be learning in spite of themselves. This, of course, also depends to a great extent on the skill of the teacher. These students come to secondary school already feeling that they are failures. Many have no desire to take part in 'school learning'. The advantage of the computer programs is that the students can take charge of their own learning – and in private! Freedom should be given to allow them to choose their own programs.

Many parents worry when they hear of school classes containing students of 'mixed ability', i.e. students are placed in classes irrespective of aptitude and ability. When every student has access to a computer this will not matter. Pupils will be able to work at their own subjects, at their own level and in their own time. Students who have 'special needs' will be given early learning programs. Students with high intellectual ability will be able to study up to (and beyond) examination standards.

If the computer has a word processing chip installed there is an even greater advantage: in most secondary schools the teaching of typing using a conventional typewriter is regarded as a CSE subject and not suitable for O-level candidates. Using the computer keyboard to teach typing gives an opportunity to less able students to 'write-out' their own work with greater emphasis on the content rather than on the skill. Gradually, over a period of time, they will begin to compare their printed-out product with books or newspapers. A dictionary program which will help them correct their spellings is an added bonus. Confidence will be built up which will have 'spin-offs' into other areas of the curriculum. Again, problem-solving programs will present them with situations that will encourage them to express themselves verbally and discuss each situation as it arises.

THE THREE Cs

CONTROL TECHNOLOGY

Control technology is one of the most exciting ways of using computers in the classroom. In Bedfordshire, the local education authority uses a bus, designed by one of their teachers, as a mobile classroom teaching control technology, using advanced equipment. In primary schools, Big Trak, Valiant Turtle, BBC Buggy, are all being used as instruments to help children understand how the computer can be programmed to control objects at some distance from the micro. The micro controls the object, but the micro is controlled by the children. Other examples include controlling traffic lights and train sets, robot arms and Lego-built cars. Fertile young imaginations can be given full rein when provided with a micro and an instrument to control. The calculation, creative stimulation, and organizational skills needed, truly help young minds to be stretched to their fullest capabilities. Children learn to experiment with equipment in the safety of a school environment. They need to work together to solve problems. They are involved, working hard rather than sitting at a desk regurgitating information given to them by a teacher out of a text book. A group of 16-year-old students won the Young Scientist of the Year award using a Commodore Pet Micro to control the stage lighting during the school's Christmas concert.

THE USE OF CONVENTIONAL AIDS AND TECHNIQUES

The use of computers in schools does not mean that conventional aids and materials are going to be ignored. They are still vitally needed in a classroom situation. The aim of all teachers is to see the all-round growth, development and maturity of the children in their care. Everything and everybody can be part of the learning situation. No one can ever be certain what is going to trigger off a learning process in a child's mind. As teachers, we aim to develop a curiosity in the children, so that they will explore the world around them and gather as much information as they can from a stimulating environment. In primary schools it is relatively easy for

102

a micro to be incorporated into a class area. It can very quickly become an integral and important piece of equipment. It does not preclude the use of all the other items usually found in schools. Art and craft, drawing, painting, collage, and pottery are still needed for the aesthetic development. The musical instruments in the school are still needed although the micro can enrich that experience. How many BBC television productions have music produced by the radiophonic workshop? *Dr Who*, to name just one. In that workshop, computers are used to coordinate the sounds that other instruments, e.g. glass bottles or shells and coconuts, make.

Audio-visual aids are used in most schools. The synchrofax machine which a few years ago was greeted with delight is now very largely stuck in stock cupboards and never sees the light of day. The sheets needed for the machine took too long to prepare and were of limited value. Televisions, slides, and videos all play an important role when a lesson is given to a group or class of children, but only the latter are becoming interactive. The advantage of the micro is self-evident when comparing it with audio-visual aids: it is interactive *now*. The child is presented with a situation on the screen and the situation will not change unless there is a response. The child must think, speak, type, test!

Secondary schools usually have more money at their disposal than do primary schools. Firms are willing to donate computers and computer accessories to schools. Most primary schools merely have cassette recorders linked to their computers. A few are luckier and have a disk drive, while a few others have bought printers with the help of private school funds. These we think are the minimum basic needs for any school. Some secondary schools have much more. Gradually other peripherals will find their way into primary schools. Large screens are invaluable if the work is for a whole class group. They allow the class a clear view and help the student to feel part of the interaction which is taking place.

As the computer technology continues to evolve, computers will increasingly be coupled to other, standard audio-visual devices. Dr Philip Barker of the Department of Computer Science at Teesside Polytechnic has developed a technique for using the micro-computer to randomly access slides on a standard slide projector.

THE THREE Cs

A more sophisticated mix of equipment can transfer a printed map onto a large piece of paper: the map is traced out onto a graphics tablet. This projects the map onto the computer screen. The screen map is used to instruct a LOGO Turtle, which draws the map on a piece of paper on the floor. The Turtle may also be used to draw blueprints or, alternatively, a map of an imaginary village. Once the streets are outlined, building blocks or Lego sets could be used to transform the plans into reality.

The above represents the more sophisticated and expensive mixes. However, one can envision simpler systems. Most important among these is coupling computer programs to books (and vice versa). The two can complement each other powerfully, as, for example, when using an illustrated dictionary to complement a set of spelling and word building programs.

In the mid-1980s, the latest technology involves 'electronic computer books' (see Plate 10). These consist of a touch-sensitive concept keyboard wired into the inside back cover of a loose-leaf notebook (attached to a computer by a cord). Any number of pages may overlie the back cover. The child merely presses down on a specific word, or part of a picture (e.g. a turtle), and the keyboard will communicate with the computer to make things happen on the computer screen. Alternatively, the computer may activate a Turtle or other robot device, a loudspeaker, a telephone, a printer, or any other peripheral. The opportunities for play and education with such a system are enormous.

BEYOND COMPUTER STUDIES

A primary class area can be an exciting environment for a young child if it is in the care of a hardworking, skilful teacher, ever ready to explore new situations and ideas. The computer is now present in the majority of schools — both primary and secondary. In the latter, micros have been in use largely in the maths area. The maths teacher was expected to take control and organize classes. These classes were designed to teach programming as a separate subject.

O-level computer studies involved studying: the history of computer development; the writing of computer programs, usually in BASIC; and the development of a project. The first program most students were presented with was a 'wage' program.

Fortunately the situation is changing and computers are being used in other subject departments. One of the first curricular areas to take advantage of the technology was Home Economics. Programs on diet content, calorific content, and menu choices became available. Similarly, other subject areas are beginning to incorporate computers into their work.

The development of language skills occurs in all areas of the curriculum. History and Geography are usually taught on a project basis. This involves a field trip to a particular place of historical or geographical importance and doing follow-up work and research as a result of the stimulus of the visit. No computer can (or should) take the place of field trips. However, the computer may be used as a data base for storing information and collecting data from every member of the trip. Such information then becomes available to all the members of the class and not just to the individual who collected the information. The creation of a class data base is another means of teaching cooperation.

Following the Norman conquest of England, William the Conqueror ordered a survey of all the properties of the realm. The resulting *Domesday Book*, a record from which there was no appeal, was completed in 1086. The 900th anniversary of this survey, in 1986, provides a superb opportunity to put computers to use in history and geography classes. 10,000 schools are to join together as part of the Domesday Project to update the statistics compiled in the eleventh century. The schools are to be joined by various departments of the BBC, the Open University, several manufacturers, and the Department of Trade and Industry. The collected information will be equivalent to two sets of *Encyclopaedia Britannica*.

Using their own computers, schools will be assigned a local area to survey. If successful, such a project will provide valuable insight into history, economics, technology, etc. – but what a marvellous educational device! Normally students are set the task of acquiring existing knowledge. Usually such a process is drab and dull. However, being able to participate in a process which creates *new* knowledge and insights – to do something of use to other people – *that* creates the sort of excitement which makes education fun.

Scientific experiments carried out in primary schools are important to allow the children to estimate, hypothesize, and test their findings. As in History and Geography, field trips are undertaken to the seaside or forest or marshland. The computer cannot replace this direct experience of our natural environment but again, if the children have visited a forest for example, the tree, insect, or animal surveys can be fed into the computer. This in no way detracts from the beautiful paintings, drawings, etc. which the children may also produce.

The joy of reading for most children is not spoilt by reading programs on the computer. Interest in reading and writing is deadened by dull, repetitive material which does not stimulate the children's imaginations. Work cards and work sheets can only be regarded as time fillers. They are only useful when carefully graded and given out to invididual children with care and knowledge of their needs and abilities.

Multi-stations will gradually appear in most schools where the programs can be centrally controlled and information can be transmitted between classes. This would be particularly useful where a whole year group is involved in a simulation exercise. Such an exercise was conducted in a comprehensive school involved with an industry project. The classes were prepared by trade unionists, managers of industries and banks, shop floor workers, etc. visiting the school. Groups were shown round various factories and given work experience. This culminated in an exercise in which each group had to organize a factory producing and selling a manufactured article. The groups had to compete with each other. Share prices, profit margins, trade union disputes, and decisions were typed into the main computer and sent to the other stations – with gratifying results.

Students studying for exams in English literature have very little chance of seeing live performances of the plays they are studying. Neither do they have the opportunity of seeing dramatizations of novels which have to be studied. With videodisks this situation will be remedied. All of Shakespeare's plays and the works of the Brontes, T.S. Eliot, Dylan Thomas, and other leading authors whose works have been dramatized for stage, screen, or television will become available on videodisk. This will bring to life the story and characterization and help students to understand some of the more obscure parts of the works. We are only at the beginning of the development of this aspect of microtechnology. As it grows and extends, so will its uses in education. However, such developments will take place only if teachers view them with excitement and interest, not with antagonism. It is the size of the education market which will determine the speed with which new systems will become available.

When a child wants some information for a piece of work, the help of a teacher or parent is sought. Information is stored in books but to get up-to-date information is rather difficult. Looking through books can be time-consuming and frustrating. Children work in the present. They do not like having to wait to find out answers. With the explosion of information technology this problem will partly be solved. PRESTEL already provides a service giving information on a wide variety of subjects. Weather forecasts, traffic hold-ups, news headlines, etc. can all be found through the pages of PRESTEL. Both BBC and ITV through CEEFAX and ORACLE provide similar information. Students need information relevant to their particular area of study. If they need information about minerals or vegetation, or if they want to compare the weather in Australia with that of South America, it should be possible to find the answers through a computer network system. Information needs to be accessible worldwide. The explosive growth of information can be daunting, but not if students are taught early enough how to be confident in handling and using it. If they are taught to use computers, data bases, and expert systems easily they will have the world at their finger tips. They will be able to call up a museum or a library in Iceland just as easily as calling up information from their teacher or parent. They will learn to consult an expert system on law or medicine with much greater ease and intelligence than we now consult a lawyer or doctor.

THE THREE Cs

LOGO is the creation of mathematician-turned-education-psychologist, Seymour Papert. Papert, working at the Massachusetts Institute of Technology, wanted to overcome the fear of maths, so frequently instilled in the average child by an incompetent education system. He developed something called 'Turtle Geometry' in which a child could make a robot turtle draw various shapes by instructing a computer (see Plate 8). The child could anticipate the turtle's movements by engaging in 'body geometry', i.e. by acting out the proposed movements. The child would need to know only a very few basic commands in order to make the computer drive the turtle.

The commands FORWARD and BACK cause the turtle to move in a straight line in the appropriate direction. These commands need to have a number added in order to specify the distance traversed. Therefore, FORWARD 20 means that the turtle will move forward 20 units (e.g. centimetres, inches, or whatever the turtle has been set at). A second set of commands causes the turtle to pivot without moving forward or backward. These commands are simply RIGHT, and LEFT, and LEFT 90 means that the turtle will turn left 90 units. If these last units are in degrees, then LEFT 90 causes the turtle to turn left 90 degrees so that it ends up facing at a right angle from its original position.

Using just two such commands, viz. FORWARD 20, LEFT 90, four times in succession would cause the turtle to create a square, twenty units on edge. The turtle would end up in the same spot as it started from, and facing in the same direction.

Such is the beauty of LOGO, that the child can now invent a new command: SQUARE. To SQUARE would consist of the commands FORWARD u, LEFT 90 repeated four times. If you want a little square, u would be a small number of units. If a large square is desired, then let u be a large number. Thus the command, SQUARE 20, would cause the turtle to draw the same square as it did above. SQUARE 40 would draw a square with each edge 40, i.e. the square would cover four times the area.

In a similar manner, a child could learn to teach the turtle how to draw a triangle, then invent the command: TRIANGLE. The same can be done with rectangles, circles, rhomboids, arcs, loops, etc., which gives the child a wide range of shapes to use as tools for drawing objects.

Let's take two simple cases. Putting a triangle on top of a square, makes it look like a house. (First attempts usually put the triangle at the side, bottom, or inside the square.) Putting a circle on top of a thin, vertical rectangle, makes it look like a tree. The child could now create two new super-commands: HOUSE and TREE. Designing trees of various shapes could lead to a super-super-command: FOREST. A mix of various shaped houses plus trees plus other designs such as bushes, walls, cars, etc. might create the super-super-super-command: STREET. In theory, the sky is the limit.

Papert wants to use the 'child as a builder'. He developed turtle geometry as a pedagogic device to allow children to build concepts in mathematics — to be precise, to have a sense of space, of movement, and of repetitive patterns which come naturally to children. Unlike Euclid's logical, and Descartes' algebraic, Papert's is a 'computational' style of geometry. Euclid's point is an entity which has a position but no other properties. Papert's turtle not only has a position, but a 'heading' as well — it faces in some direction. This is a concept wholly familiar to children, as for example in 'I'm here. I'm facing the window'. For Papert, 'body geometry' is crucial in forming a link with the more orthodox formal geometry. It is also a method for developing more formal skills and logic. Since it is the child who commands, the child experiences the pleasure of controlling an object in its environment. It learns to build upon routines as naturally as it learns to speak. The branching nature of the computer program allows the child to string a series of commands, to draw a square or a triangle, or, as we have discussed above, to go to a STREET or a CITY or a COUNTRY.

The power of this learning technique is that it encourages children to attempt complex tasks by reducing them to a series of small, 'mind-sized' bites. Thus analysis and synthesis become second nature to the children. Equally important is the fact that children develop a natural and healthy attitude towards mistakes. Mistakes are inevitable when trying to do something new. They are not something to be ashamed of. Rather they are mere 'bugs' which need to be uncovered and corrected.

We will have further comments to make on the work of Mike Sharples and his use of LOGO for teaching literacy skills in a later chapter (Chapter 11). What should be stressed at this point is that programs like LOGO, word processing, and data base programs constitute the sort of 'content-free' software which allows students to exercise their creative imagination and develop their own information skills. At the moment these programs are limited by the power of the hardware which usually lacks sufficient memory to do these programs full justice. In addition, many teachers are not yet aware of the enormous potential of these open-ended systems.

HOW DOES A TEACHER GET STARTED?

There cannot be a teacher who now is not aware of microcomputers. Many, however, are either not interested or are afraid. To those who are interested but don't know how to get started, we advise: talk to friends. Others may be in the same boat. Ask colleagues – don't overlook education advisers and teacher resource centres. With luck, you might uncover a friendly computer buff in your school, willing to help. Browse in bookstores and peruse the magazine racks of large shops. There are many books and periodicals to help. In fact, the massive growth in the personal computer magazine industry is phenomenal. In 1974 there was only one magazine, now the newsagents' shelves are full of them and more are appearing each week. Another approach is to attend lectures or conferences or to take a course offered by a local college or other institution. There is no excuse for any teacher to remain ignorant. However, the best way to overcome computerphobia is to buy a home computer. And the best place to overcome computer ignorance is in the privacy of one's own home. Our advice is: buy a computer which you can afford and which has sufficient software to help you stay one step ahead. Needless to say, buy the model most likely to relate to the one used in your classroom. (For example, in the UK, the BBC is widely used in the school system. If you cannot afford the BBC, buy the Electron which is sufficiently similar to allow you to develop the expertise needed to work with the BBC).

THE ELM SYSTEM

Once a teacher has become familiar with the computer, to the point of being able to connect it to various kinds of hardware such as tape recorders, printers, joysticks, or other peripherals (a skill which can easily be acquired within an hour), then it becomes time to badger the Head to purchase an Electronic Learning Machine (ELM) [1] system (see Plate 9). ELM, produced by Format Peripherals Ltd is designed for the BBC 'B' micro and incorporates a stereo cassette tape which allows the visual material of the computer to be recorded on one track while the teacher's voice can be recorded simultaneously on the other. Text and sound are completely synchronized once the material has been recorded. Central to the system is the ELM keyboard which provides 300 extra characters in addition to the usual letters, numbers, and punctuation marks. The visual track is created simply by typing on to the screen. The keyboard, using one of four overlays, allows a teacher to use over 100 Maths or Science symbols, over 100 graphics shapes to build up diagrams, and special characters for French, German, Italian, and Spanish. The teacher has a choice of colours, enlarged text, and underlining. The voice is added by talking into a microphone, while a moving marker on the screen allows exact synchronization with the text or diagram. Note that this system *requires no prior knowledge of programming* to create lessons (utilizing the teacher's voice) on the computer.

From here on in, children will use computers whether we will it or not. The computers will be as much a part of their lives as television and pocket calculators. One or two lessons on the computer, prepared by you, with your voice on the cassette player, is bound to have a favourable impact on your pupils. A teacher and pupils working together, to develop proper use of the new technology, will create a sense of accomplishment and pride which will more than repay the extra time and effort invested in this process.

THE THREE Cs

Schools should prepare children for the future. At the same time, we want children to learn about, and to cope with, the present. The ability to speak, argue, discuss, and communicate with other people is of paramount importance. No other educational tool can help teachers more in these vital tasks than can the computer. Teachers will need to be open-minded and eager to accept computers into their classrooms. They need not be capable of doing every subject their pupils excel in. They only need to accept the fact that they and their students have at their fingertips a world of information which can be used to educate themselves and others.

Chapter 9
Slow Learners, Handicapped Children, and Talented Children

Modern education is highly institutionalized. No longer is education left to the family − as it once was. Instead, hundreds of millions of children around the world are crammed into systems which try to teach them reading, writing, and arithmetic, as well as the other skills necessary for surviving in an industrial civilization. Such massive efforts carried out at a national level require checks and balances which place the vast majority of children into straitjackets of curricula and examinations. Only a relatively small number of children escape the system. Most of these, end up in special education.

Because special education is tailored, at least in theory, to children with special needs, it tends to be much more flexible. And because it is more flexible − because it is not as encumbered with fixed curricula or examinations − it is easier to experiment in the *special*, than within the general, education system. It becomes much easier to try out new things in special education. For this reason, as far as the use of computers is concerned, if one wants to know what is likely to be happening in education five to ten years from now, one should look at what's happening in special education now.

In the UK, the Warnock Report of 1978 [1], identifies 'children with special needs' to include the 'blind, partially blind, deaf, partially deaf, educationally sub-normal, epileptic, maladjusted, physically handicapped, speech defective and delicate'. The Warnock Report goes on to point out that: 'Regardless of the cause of such children's problems, family or social, unless part of their

113

educational provision is designed to compensate for the deprivation they have suffered, they will be unable to benefit from education in the ordinary sense'.

It should not be inferred that prior to the report no help was being given to these children. Far from it. There have been schools, special schools, assessment classes, and hospital schools to help educate children who have special needs, for many years. The trouble is that at present, children with severe problems are far removed from normal schools and are educated separately. The extent of this segregation is illustrated by a student teacher who described her feeling after visiting such an establishment. 'I had mixed feelings about my visit to a hospital school. What type of children were taught in the school? Were all of them educated or just some? The visits to the school really opened my eyes. I saw a wide range of handicapped children, physically, mentally, psychiatrics, orthopaedics, being educated as far as their capabilities would allow. One thing that did strike me was that not all physically handicapped children were mentally handicapped. They were slower than their peers in normal schools but that can probably be put down to the fact that their lives were constantly disrupted by visits to the hospital school and home. I saw children who were spending anything from two days to twelve weeks in hospital as well as some who were spending all their lives there.' The surprise of an educated student teacher that physically handicapped children were not necessarily mentally handicapped is illustrative of the attitude that people hold in general. Most people tend to turn a blind eye to or are frightened of people who are 'different'. The Warnock Committee recommends that: '. . . firm links should be established between special and ordinary schools in the same vicinity'.

Warnock considers that 16 per cent of children need special educational provision but that only one-eighth of this group should be educated outside normal schools.

As soon as microcomputers became available as an educational tool, teachers of children with special needs began developing programs and peripherals for use in special education. This occurred all over the world. For example, at Yamanashi University in Japan, deaf children were being taught to speak by using a model of the mouth and throat to show how sounds are produced [2]. In Australia, blind children were helped by computerized braille producers [3].

In the United States, E. Paul Goldenberg's work at MIT represents some of the most profound and sensitive basic work in the field. His book *Special Technology for Special Children* [4] is a classic in the field and should be required reading for all therapists and special education teachers. As part of Seymour Papert's LOGO group, Goldenberg used the computer to help in all aspects of special education. For deaf children, Goldenberg concludes that the greatest value of the computer is that it is: '. . . a flexible and growing source of intellectual stimulation that encourages, but does not depend on, social communication'. We will discuss other aspects of Goldenberg's work, but what he says here about the computer and deaf children may be generalized for all handicapped children, and in fact for *all children*. It has equal validity for adults as well, including those afflicted by disease or accident who thereby suffer physical, mental, or emotional incapacity. As a major extension of a person's ability to communicate, as well as a source of entertainment and stimulation, the computer will prove to be one of the great therapeutic devices of the century.

In the UK the National Council for Special Education (Stratford-upon-Avon) published in 1984 a booklet entitled: *Microcomputers and Special Educational Needs: A Guide to Good Practice* by Bob Hogg [5]. This 57-page booklet is crammed with useful information for British teachers; it includes an excellent set of references and two pages of 'Useful Addresses'. The Schools Council Report (1982), *Microcomputers in Special Education*, by F. Green, R. Hart, C. McCall, and I. Staples, provides a useful overview including charts and diagrams which match specific applications of the microcomputer to meeting special education needs [6]. However, the most useful thing a teacher in Britain can do is to call on one of the four Special Education Microelectronic Resource Centres (SEMERCs). The addresses are listed in Appendix E. The SEMERCs, which were set up and supported by the UK Government's Microcomputers in Education Program (MEP), produce a newsletter and other published material and reports. We have been particularly impressed by Bob Dyke, the Manager of the North-Western Region located at Manchester Polytechnic. His lectures and demonstrations of a variety of microcomputer-controlled toys and other educational devices are highly professional and entertaining. Such toys are electrically operated by switches activated by touch, changing body position, breathing hard in or out, pointing with a finger, foot pressure, grasping, or any vocal noise. They light up, play music, and jump about. We liked particularly a teddy bear that banged cymbals together whenever activated by any of the means described above. Another impressive demonstration is of a device for teaching deaf children to speak by showing them on the computer screen a train which will puff and move forward only when the right sound is produced.

For example, if a 'sh' sound is produced it moves forwards, but a 'th' sound would not produce the desired effect.

USING A ROBOT TURTLE

Dyke is one of a cadre of dedicated and imaginative workers emerging all over the world, striving to improve the lot of handicapped children. We would like to describe here the experiences of two of our students, Paul Quintas and David Kirby. Quintas took a 'Valiant Turtle' robot into a local school for severely mentally handicapped children. There was no question of teaching these children LOGO, or how to use a computer. Instead, a specially designed 'concept' keyboard (see Glossary) was used to command the turtle. This concept keyboard, devised by Kirby, consisted of a set of nine large switches. The switches were arranged in a 3 by 3 format. The whole board could be overlaid with plastic or paper sheets. These could have whatever symbols a teacher would like to see appear in each of the nine positions.

One of the first problems to emerge was that some of the children did not associate the board with the turtle. Several did not comprehend that they could command the turtle by pressing the keys on the board. Secondly, many of the children had no conception of pressing a key only once, but would simply keep pressing down. Thirdly, even though the keys were relatively large and well separated, there was still a considerable tendency to press more than one key simultaneously. With some children, the task proved to be too much. It became clear that the only way to get them interested at all would involve the use of a single switch. This could be accomplished by having the keyboard have all nine switches perform the same function. No matter where the child pressed, the action would be the same. Having a lot of noise and flashing lights associated with the turtle, also helps.

A few of the children, however, worked with the turtle quite well and demonstrated some surprising instances of lateral thinking. For example, one child had no clue how to make the turtle turn but tried the method of simply turning the board 90°, then pressing FORWARD with a view that that would change the direction of the turtle. Of course, given the system, it didn't. However, this experience did suggest designing a new device: a concept keyboard attached to a steering wheel so that as you turn the concept keyboard, the turtle turns with it.

What did work, was labelling the left flipper with a prominent piece of red tape, and the right flipper with a prominent piece of green tape, then labelling the concept board keys so that the three keys on the left (in the first column) were bright red and the three keys on the right side (in the third column) were labelled a bright green. Whenever the red or the green keys were pressed, the turtle would turn 15° (left or right). To make it turn at a full right angle, the same key would have to be pressed six separate times. Using this system as well as an arrow forward at the top centre position, and an arrow downward at the bottom centre position, allowed the child to make the turtle move forward, backward and turn. Asking a child to use the turtle to knock down a pile of toy bricks elicited great excitement and entertainment.

Unfortunately, it was not possible to continue this investigation in any great detail. However, we might discuss some of the theoretical possibilities for teaching very young children and severely mentally handicapped children. One would begin with nine keys, all of which contain arrows facing up. No matter which key the child pushed, the turtle would move forward, let's say 20 centimetres. If the turtle caught his or her attention, the child might push a key whenever he or she wished the turtle to move. The child would learn that pushing the keyboard has an effect on the turtle. That's an important insight: you are able to make something happen at a distance. Normally, this insight must come fairly early in infancy. It must be crucial for motivating a child to engage in further learning and experimentation.

The next step is to put on the concept keyboard only one arrow and leave the other eight spaces blank. The turtle now moves only when the child presses the space with the arrow. It is important to move the arrow to the various positions at random, so that the child understands it is the arrow, rather than the location on the board, which is important for activating the turtle. When that lesson has been clearly learned, and the child pushes the arrow whenever it wants the turtle to move, the time is ripe for introducing a second set of commands. These should consist of the coloured tape markings which Quintas found so useful. On the front flippers of the turtle a bright coloured patch is placed (red on the left, green on the right) and the corresponding colours are put on two of the keys, one on the left-hand side of the board, and the other on the right-hand side. The child now learns that if the arrow is pressed the turtle goes forward, if the red on the left-hand side is pressed the turtle turns left, and if the green is pressed the turtle turns right. When these lessons have been learned, it becomes appropriate to introduce a backward arrow, or some other symbol, which now allows the child full manoeuvrability of the turtle. The final set of commands involves lifting the pen up, or letting it down, so that the child can now begin to draw things using the turtle.

Of great help in developing the above system is the 'Electronic Computer Colour Book', originally designed for the TRS-80. It looks like a regular three-hole notebook binder. However, the inside of the book cover is divided into 12 squares in a 3 by 4 format. Each square is numbered (1–12) and represents an individual switch. The notebook has a cord and a plug which allows it to be plugged into the joystick port of the computer (see Plate 10).

Into this notebook the teacher or parent inserts three-hole, loose-leaf pages which may contain twelve letters, numbers, symbols, or pictures. The whole notebook may be filled with pages. Such is the beauty of the design that even an entire telephone book placed on top of the switches will still allow pressing the top page at any given site to cause the appropriate switch to be operated. This means that the notebook filled with pages may be opened to any page, and the top page (on the right-hand side) will be ready for action. All the parent or teacher need do is type the page number into the computer so as to activate the software. Actually, the child may be taught to carry out this simple procedure − in some cases using the book itself.

At the time of writing a BBC version of the 'Electronic Computer Colour Book' coupled to the 'Valiant Turtle' was under development to help teach very young, or handicapped, children the rudiments of turtle control. The book and software are sufficiently cheap to allow virtually all turtle owners to purchase them, so that it should be of great help to institutions and individuals engaged in special education.

Once the rudiments of turtle control have been mastered, the child can begin to enter the world of LOGO.

Considering that the child merely needs to push keys or use one of the other systems described above, it is able to draw pictures, letters, numbers, etc. and a whole world can begin to open up. There is an even more important psychological aspect to this procedure. Handicapped children are always having things done for them or to them. The ability to make something happen 'out there' is a source of enormous satisfaction. The idea of having a robot slave following your commands is of enormous positive value to the self-image and development of a child.

THE MAKATON SYSTEM

An entirely different aspect of using a concept keyboard for disabled children is exemplified by the work of David Kirby. His system was designed to provide a method for a non-verbal person to communicate with others. The primary aim of the project was to produce a computer system, using the MAKATON symbols, which could be integrated into a language and communication scheme for people incapable of normal speech.

The MAKATON system consists of a vocabulary which has been specially designed to provide a controlled method of teaching the British Sign Language (BSL) to mentally retarded children and adults, and to other language-handicapped people. This language provides a basic means of communication, encourages expressive speech, and develops an understanding of language through the visual medium of the signs and logical structure. The MAKATON system was originally devised by Margaret Walker (Senior Speech Therapist at Botleys Park Hospital, Chertsey, Surrey) and Cathy Johnston and Tony Cornforth (Psychiatric Hospital Visitors) from the Royal Association of the Deaf and Dumb. In the late 1960s, staff from the Royal Association (RADD) working in the Surrey Hospitals for the mentally ill and the mentally handicapped, highlighted the problem of the deaf, mentally handicapped residents, completely isolated because of their inability to communicate. Simple attempts were made to introduce some signing and the deaf residents responded eagerly.

In the early 1970s, RADD was invited to introduce signing to a group of deaf residents at Botleys Park Hospital and it was here that Margaret Walker joined the team and carried out a research project to evaluate the use of British Sign Language with a group of deaf, mentally handicapped residents. The results of this early project showed convincingly that BSL could be learned easily by mentally handicapped people, and also that it could be used as a tool in the teaching of language.

The MAKATON vocabulary was subsequently expanded to include approximately 350 words/signs which were to be learned in eight stages, with a ninth stage for a specialized additional vocabulary. Each stage contained about 35 to 40 words. The vocabulary was designed to be small and limited, yet contain enough words to comprise a useful basic vocabulary. It was also essential that it would follow the development of language, and that it would be appropriate for mentally handicapped people. Lastly, it

STAGE 1

mummy	daddy	brother	sister	nurse
doctor	drink (cup)	biscuit	dinner	toilet
bed	chair	table	house (home)	car (bus)
I (me)	you	where	what	here
there	please (thank you)	eat (food)	look (see)	stand up
sit	wash	bath	go	come
give	good	bad	yes	no

121

needed to be selected in such a way that the signs would easily combine into short phrases.

The MAKATON vocabulary has become the system used in the majority of Educationally Special Schools in Great Britain. It is used for:

(1) Mentally handicapped deaf and non-deaf children and adults who have little or no expressive speech and poor comprehension.

(2) People who are both mentally and physically handicapped.

(3) Those considered to be autistic.

(4) Some young deaf children in the ordinary range of intelligence.

(5) Children with severe articulation or speech rhythm problems who need a temporary alternative.

(6) Certain normal adults with acquired speech problems.

Those who teach and use the system include speech therapists, teachers, occupational therapists, psychologists, parents, instructors, and school and hospital staff. Experience has shown that, in addition to the development of concepts and language, other positive results occur − increased eye contact and improvement in attention, sociability, vocalization, and expressive speech. A marked reduction in inappropriate behaviour is also reported. For those with severe communication impediments, signing can stimulate (rather than interfere with) language development.

Communication and language covers speech, natural gesture, signing, the use of symbols, and body language. MAKATON appears to be the only alternative communication system which has been divided into developmental stages on a hierarchical basis. This is the key feature in any teaching program for people with severe learning difficulties. The 350, or so, terms provide a core communications system similar to those uncovered by research into mentally handicapped adults. The MAKATON vocabulary is frequently self-explanatory. For example, the sign and symbol for the word 'chair' are distilled from the sitting position. This type of concrete reinforcement is essential when developing language programs for children with severe learning difficulties.

The computer system developed by David Kirby provides a series of programs developed over an 18-month period, initially while Mr Kirby was working for the Walsall Education Authority. The system uses a specially designed concept keyboard since the traditional Qwerty keyboard presents an enormous obstacle to people who have severe learning difficulties. The concept keyboard merely requires a touch to gain the response. The keys are not only relatively large, but will respond to fingers that keep pressing long after the initial push. The system can also be operated by using a Single Switch which is connected to the User Port of the BBC microcomputer. The system works with the BBC model B, which is the one most likely to be found in British special schools during the mid-1980s. The system is designed to work with a Disk Filing System which provides an open and flexible program. This allows teachers the chance to develop their own teaching routines by designing different overlays made of plastic or paper. What appears on the screen is easily programmed in by the teacher using simple commands to the computer. The format of the screen is designed to follow closely the format of the teaching material which the children will be using, either in the classroom or in their own private tuition.

The symbols on the keyboard are presented on the screen by the computer. The cursor of the computer moves across the screen, one by one touching each of these various symbols or pictures. The child can depress a single switch to stop the cursor at whatever location on the screen it wishes. One of the earliest programs, therefore, is to get the child to match a symbol or picture on the keyboard with the corresponding symbol or picture on the screen. Matching symbols or pictures is therefore the first of the series of exercises. In due course that can be extended to match the pictures with symbols, then with words. In this way the meaning of the MAKATON vocabulary is slowly taught. Whenever the child achieves the correct response there is a reward routine on the computer. In due course, the child will be able to move the cursor and access pictures to create phrases and sentences by combining words such as 'Daddy car' or 'Mummy dinner'. These could then be read out, or spoken by a voice chip. If a printer is available, it could be printed out for the child to keep.

THE THREE Cs

Mr Kirby field-tested the system at a number of institutions, including one in which the children had severe multiple difficulties. The teachers reported that when using the system the children were highly motivated and gained confidence quickly. The children went through some of the stages of 'recognition', 'matching', and 'sequencing'. They did not need to complete the 'recognition' stage for all the symbols before proceeding to the 'matching' sections of the scheme. The children found that it was easy to generalize the symbols they knew. Thus, they were able to understand the computer symbol for 'Mummy' if they had previously learned the MAKATON symbol for 'Mummy'. The teacher was able to use the system flexibly and design his own teaching routines. The system allowed an up-dating of any file simply by instructing it to store new sets or combinations of symbols. The hardware enabled the children to access the symbols independently, if they could work the more complex switches. However, a great deal of work could also be carried out by the multiple handicapped children who were able to access the symbols using only a single switch.

Coupled to other devices and systems which are emerging throughout the world, one can begin to hope for an extraordinary improvement in the ability of handicapped children both to communicate with the outside world and to learn its mysteries. Handicapped children are trapped in the prison of their handicap. The computer is the key to their escape.

SLOW LEARNERS IN THE MAINSTREAM OF EDUCATION

Children can be very cruel. They can gibe at handicapped children, increasing their feelings of failure. Computers can be a great help in this situation. For example, two boys aged nine were allowed to write a story using a word processing facility on the BBC. One had severe learning difficulties and, in fact, had to go on to a special school. The other had severe writing problems and still needs special tuition. At the time, they were reluctant to write the story and spent some time talking about it. They then wrote the following story.

124

```
        When The Plane Crashed


We    where    on    a    plane  andthe
junlgel  was    blurw  us.      Then
the    plane    lost    contrl      and
the plane was goring down into
the        junlgel.   Then     eveybod
scird    put    yor    sit    bets on.
Then  the  plane  crashed          in
the    junlgel  and  Roy  and  Terry
where    the    tow    svars    and    a
shehpat  gim  to  get  us  home.


            Aged  9  and  10
               Class  8
            March  1984
```

The result and their sense of achievement was much better than anything we could have hoped for. The rest of the class did not comment on the poor spelling and other mistakes, but got into the spirit of the story. For once, the two boys felt that they had accomplished something: they had written a story which looked neat, tidy, presentable, and told a tale of interest to the others.

Children who experience difficulty with maths can use easier maths programs and work through them more slowly. We find that once children are using a computer program, most of the rest of the class carry on working at their own level. They are quite content knowing that eventually their turn will come. However, it does require careful grading on the teacher's part to ensure that the children are working at the appropriate level of difficulty. The open-ended maths program, the use of robot devices such as Big Track, or even better, the Valiant Turtle, all allow children of whatever level of intelligence to work at their own pace. Children with learning difficulties may only program the turtle to move forward or backward. More able or talented children can produce more complicated instructions. With these sorts of activities, there is much less chance of fingers pointing in derision, or boasts about which maths is being plodded through.

Some time in the future, when all schools are linked to a PRESTEL-type system, children will be able to access information for their own needs. It will be possible to create a greater variety of individual learning situations, especially if the child also has a computer at home. This means, increasingly, that education can be tailored to individual children in a classroom situation.

Maladjusted children usually have great difficulty in concentrating for long periods, and yet when they are teenagers it is usually expected of them. Simulation exercises and life skill programs, which we will discuss in greater detail in Chapter 11, will help them settle. For example, Heather Govier has developed software to teach 'Survival Skills'. These range from 'Road Tests' which help to develop knowledge of road signs, to core curriculum programs. Adventure games on 'Life Choices', develop social skills. Frequently, these children have so many problems of their own that to escape into the fictional world of a computer game is probably highly desirable. It could enhance both their willingness and their ability to learn.

Maladjusted children can create such problems in a classroom that they have to be sent to special schools, or hospital units. Here the more favourable staffing ratios in such units allow the children to attain the attention they deserve. However, in such groups, there may be a wide age range and a wide range of problems. Such a group might include an anorexic girl, a suicidal boy, and a child suffering from school phobia. These children need to be educated individually. A computer for each child with an individual schedule of learning is, obviously, at least part of the answer.

Gradually, programs are appearing which cover most areas of 'special need' such as remedial reading, creative writing, and money management skills. Once the problems are diagnosed and the educational provisions detailed, it should be possible for these children to carry on their education, no matter where they are. With a computer at home, at school, and in the hospital school, there will exist a continuity of experience and learning which has not been previously possible. With improved medical care and more effective drug therapy, children will need to spend less time in hospital. Microtechnology will help these children learn at their own pace and in their own time. If they are unwell one day, they will not miss out on a piece of learning. The computer will wait patiently until they are ready to resume again.

TALENTED CHILDREN

If an estimated 16 per cent of children have special educational needs of a remedial nature, it is equally important to ask about the educational provision for talented children. The Warnock Report made the recommendation that: 'Long term studies should be made on the needs and achievements of gifted children ... we cannot afford to waste their talents ...' [7].

Three areas of 'giftedness' are generally recognised:

(1) Those who are generally recognized by their schools as possessing superior all-round intellectual ability, confirmed where possible by individual testing.
(2) Those who exhibit a markedly superior developmental level of performance and achievement which has been reasonably consistent over the years.
(3) Those for whom fairly confident predictions can be made as to continual rapid progress towards outstanding achievement, either in academic areas, or in music, sport, dance, or art, and whose abilities are not primarily attributable to purely physical development.

127

THE THREE Cs

In the USA, special classes for the talented have existed for some time. Talented sportsmen are frequently granted large scholarships to American universities. In China, Russia, and some other countries, athletes, particularly gymnasts who will take gold medals at international meetings, are identified at a very young age. Such talented young children are set aside from the others to attend special schools and classes to help them excel. The Bolshoi Ballet auditions students before the age of ten years. If they pass the audition they are then expected to take up residence in Moscow. There they work to clearly defined schedules, going home only once a year.

In the UK there are special schools for talented children, especially in the field of music. The Yedudi Menuhin School, the Manchester College of Music, various cathedral choir schools, all are centres of excellence. Unfortunately, they tend to be for the minority of students only. 'The majority of us believe that the English primary education at its best is better adapted than any other we have seen to provide for the needs of the gifted individual without segregating him' (Warnock). Whilst we would agree with this statement, the comment 'at its best', is worthy of comment. What about the schools which are not good? – schools where the staff are limited by a lack of facilities; schools not in a position to help talented youngsters. What about schools situated in deprived areas – inner-city schools – where it takes all the energies of the teacher to cope with social problems? How have these teachers the time to work out individual programs of learning for talented youngsters?

While computers cannot and should not be considered a universal panacea, it would be possible (as in the case of remedial children) to provide individual learning systems. Talented children can progress at their own pace in their own particular area of expertise. Alternatively, a talented artist may be able to work at the computer merely to master the other basic subjects such as maths and science, then spend the rest of the day painting, sculpting, practising the flute, or whatever. Thus, it will be possible for these students to spend less time on the basics (using a computer), and more time developing their talents. Footballers, cricketers, and athletes can spend their mornings learning the basic subjects and their afternoons being coached at sports centres.

Slow Learners, Handicapped Children, and Talented Children

It used to be accepted that, in order to be a top-flight footballer, it was necessary to leave school at sixteen years to concentrate on football. It was widely broadcast and commented on a few years ago when a player for Liverpool Football Club had a university degree. This should not be unusual. It should, in fact, be the norm.

The Plowden Report of 1966 commented on talented children: 'Their handwriting is often behind their mental development'. Their minds seem to work quicker than their fingers. Word processing on the computer should overcome that problem as well as the problem of the illegible scrawl. Talented children will be able to tap more readily into the global information store. Future doctors, scientists, musicians will use computers to discover the world and keep up to date with the latest developments. Whatever the quality or degree of talent a child possesses, it should be possible to develop that talent to the fullest extent while not hindering the development of other, perhaps more ordinary, skills.

We would like to conclude this chapter by citing the case of Tony Cains.

From the day Tony first started school it was obvious that he was one of those gifted children referred to in the reports we discussed above. At 4½ years old he could read, wasn't particularly interested in playing, and could carry on 'adult' conversations with clarity and an extensive vocabulary. Sitting at a table for any length of time was onerous – he loved to explore the environment. Mathematics interested him but he hated to record his findings. He loved to build Meccano bridges or other forms of construction – mechanics were second nature to him. He always tried to make things move. Once involved in experimenting he would become excited, talking rapidly, moving from one area of the experiment to the other, testing, probing, delighted when his predictions proved correct, but if they didn't, merely taking time out for a rethink.

Friendships did not materialize until he was 9 years old, and then with older children – an obvious sign of a talented child. Once he found a friend, the friendship lasted a long time. With many talented children there is always a dilemma: intellectually, they ought to be placed with older children; however, removing them from their age peers can cause adverse social effects and create emo-

THE THREE Cs

Tony Cains   Computer:Video Genie   Born:8.2.70

I started computing in the third year at Junior school using a Commodore P.E.T. borrowed from the local Teacher's Centre.A group of around twenty used it as part of our maths lessons.This is when I learned to program - first on paper,then "hands on".At first all my programs were mathematical but I soon wrote a Moon Lander game.
I went on a course about "Problem Solving using Computers" in the fourth year.
When I was eleven my father bought a Video Genie for me to use at home because we knew that the local comprehensive school did not offer computer studies as an option. The Video Genie is a cheap Japanese copy of the Tandy TRS 80 with 16K of memory and an integral cassette recorder.I use it with a twelve inch black and white television and I think it is better than the P.E.T.
I think my uses of the computer can be divided into four groups:
1. Revision : For spelling tests,chemical formulae, foreign vocabulary tests.
2. General Education : Maths Tables,Graphs,Pythagorian trianges,Factorisation and Quadratic Equations.
3. Games : I have many games written by myself that I play quite a bit,plus four commercial games.I play Sargon Chess a lot but it can beat me on the easiest level!
4. General Purpose : Working on programs either just "for programing's sake" or prgrams to do just one job - draw patterns,solve problems - that I often erase afterwards.

When I was 13 I added high-resolution graphics,48K more memory,a disk drive and a printer.
After this I used the computer much as before,only more so,but with the added advantage of being able to keep a permernant record of screen displays using a screen dump utility I wrote.
The addition of a printer and disk drive has enabled me to use the computer for a fifth catagory - as an *Electronic Secretary*.This includes word processing,keeping lists such as my Meccano parts and writing large numbers of Beetle cards.The only snag with the word processor is that it cannot correct spelling!.
I don't find the lack of colour much of a drawback,as colour is used mainly for games.
One big advantage of a computer is that because it can perform repetitive calculations very easily,it can solve complex mathematical problems using the "suck it and see" method which involves trying thousands of different values until you find one that fits.
I am now in my fourth year at Comprehensive school and I have at last started to do computer studies.The school has nine BBC Micros and one of the chemistry teachers takes seven of us once a week after school to do computer studies.I will have to write a program on my own computer to submit for the exam.
As well as the BBCs the school has an RML 380Z with twin disk drives that no-one really knows how to use.I am the resident expert on it but it is rarely used now.
I also help out my friends when they have computer trouble - I recently explained to two boys how to use the graphics on their Commodore 64 which they had had for around seven months without being able to understand it.
I am a member of NATGUG - the NATional Trs 80 and Genie Users Group,and I recently obtained some programs from them.

Now that I have had my computer for over three and a half years,it has lost its novelty value .I would now like to enter the field of robotics with an interface and Meccano robots.I can see myself following a career in computer based high-technology design when I leave university

130

tional problems — problems which may linger for a lifetime.

As we indicated, in the future a computer-based education system should provide individual learning systems. Classes will contain once again, as in Victorian times, mixed-age groups. Tony represents the future. His father bought him a computer when he was eleven. At the time of this writing he was fourteen. A copy of his story as he wrote it on his word processor, is shown on page 130.

Chapter 10
Computers in the Home (for Parents only)

Childhood is a recent phenomenon. In rich families, babies used to be placed in the care of nannies and were not expected to be noticed until they were ready to take their place in the adult world. In poorer families they were expected to work from a very early age. As recently as this century, there were four-year-old children in Britain working in mines. Fortunately this situation has changed dramatically and childhood is accepted as an important stage of growth and development. It is understood that a deprived or unhappy childhood can lead to serious problems in adult life. Conversely, a happy stimulating childhood can lead to a happy secure maturity. This latter stage is what we all desire for our children. How we as parents help our children is fundamental to their development.

Heredity, intelligence, environment, and education directly affect how children grow and mature. There is nothing parents can do about the first two factors, but they can have either a stimulating or deadening effect on the latter two. It is probably true to say that an early, stimulating environment, coupled with a good education, can more than compensate for deficiencies caused by heredity or innate intelligence. All but the most severely handicapped children learn how to talk. That in itself is an extraordinary intellectual feat. Given that much 'innate' intelligence, children can be stimulated and educated so that their 'effective' intelligence develops to become on a par even with gifted children. As we have pointed out before, the average teenager today understands the world much better than the wisest of minds of the ancient world. Furthermore, all children are good at some things.

The delight with which parents greet a new-born baby has to be experienced to be understood. Similarly, the responsibilities that this baby brings has also to be experienced to be understood. No books, lectures, or advice can truly prepare parents for the changes a baby makes to their lives, especially the first-born. Caring parents always have, and will want to help their children. Many parents do not always know how to set about helping their offspring. This is not necessarily a hindrance – so much of the information youngsters learn pre-school seems to have been soaked through the pores of their skin. Sometimes forcing children, for example, to correctly pronounce words before they are ready, or showing signs of irritation when a child struggles to find a word, can lead to the development of a stammer. As parents we have to create a stimulating environment in which our children will learn. This does not mean setting out a room as a classroom, far from it. Many parents do not realize the educational environment they have already created in the colour, the style, the books, and the furniture of their home. Even the locality of the home is important. An inner city child sees large shops, and apartment blocks. A child from a rural area learns about animals, farms, and the countryside. They learn from experience. It is up to the parents to help their children gain as wide an experience of life as possible. Side by side with this experience is the ability to talk through and about whatever experiences they encounter, incidental or manufactured.

A very young baby does not understand the words spoken by siblings or parents in their presence. This does not prevent the baby from reacting to the voice. A crying baby in a room alone will stop, even if it is only momentarily, when a voice is heard. Similarly a stimulating environment is a learning environment. It is up to us, as parents, to realize the effect home has on our children.

People are the greatest teachers. The way they talk, move, act and react in any situation is watched by young children. Very young children imitate their parents and other adults. If a great deal of conversation is heard at home a child will quickly learn to speak with ease and fluency. If parents are interested in sport a child will show equal interest. If parents are aggressive and use bad language children will do likewise. Once a child can talk, the stream of questions can be interminable and unanswerable. It requires a great deal of patience to cope with the volume of talk. Nevertheless talking must be encouraged and extended.

Research [1] has shown that a child who sees parents read will want to read. They will copy Mum and pick up the paper to see what is on television. This is an important stage in learning to read. The child realizes that a newspaper contains information. Favourite books are read over and over again until they are learned by heart. Parents can extend this by asking pertinent questions – How? What? Where? When? – encouraging the children to think.

Children should be allowed to bake. 'Reading' the recipes, weighing the ingredients, timing the food in the oven – these are all learning experiences. They are of more value than learning the tables by rote. A visit to the shops is valuable. Reading the labels to see the ingredients, or the country of origin – being allowed to buy a loaf of bread, counting out the money given and the change received, are all learning situations. Choosing what to buy with pocket money is not only a mathematical experience but a problem-solving situation. Children must learn independence. Allowing them time and money to spend as they like, encourages them towards solving a problem and gives them a measure of independence.

If you allow children to plant seeds, either in a garden or in a box, they will be learning about the natural world – caring for the seeds, reading the instructions, observing the growth, measuring the plants, talking about the conditions needed to help them grow. Children have a great sense of wonder when they see their seeds producing plants. It is an aesthetic experience which will help them appreciate their world.

There is no need to spend vast sums of money on musical instruments for children to make music. Peas in a tin, glass jars with various amounts of water, pan lids – all provide satisfactory musical tones for children. They will very happily 'play along' with the music from a radio or record player. Again, such play gives them an aesthetic experience and also allows them to be creative.

Mud, snow, waste paper, glue, scissors, paints, pencils, crayons can give enormous pleasure to most children. It depends on the attitude of the parents. If they prevent or dislike the messes caused by a child playing with such materials, a wide area of creativity and imaginative play will be missed. When children play with cardboard boxes they become castles or space rockets, or a baby's cradle or a house. The possibilities are endless. The only restriction is in the mind of the child. Scissors, waste paper, and glue can keep a child happy for a long time and can give great satisfaction. Asking questions can provoke interesting responses. On being asked, 'Tell me about your painting', a teacher was told by a five-year-old, 'I can't because I don't know what it is until I have finished'. On the other hand, another child gave a long detailed description of a cat being chased up a tree by a dog and a fire engine being called to rescue the unfortunate pet.

The boundless energy children have can be very wearing on parents. Being able to channel it to everyone's satisfaction is a skill to be developed. Running, jumping, climbing are vital to the physical development of a healthy child. Learning to swim is vital both for safety and enjoyment. Noisy, boisterous games on the floor or in the park can be fun and necessary.

Equally important is peace and quiet. Sitting on a parent's knee listening to a story or a piece of music allows the children to experience peace of mind. Usually children have to be taught this skill of sitting quietly. If they have had a stimulating day and a fun time in the bath they will be quite happy to sit and listen. It doesn't matter to a child if mum or dad sings out of tune. It is the physical and loving contact which gives the rest and satisfaction.

Discipline can be difficult. Too much and a child becomes repressed. Too little and a child becomes uncontrollable and an unhappy child. Children need the security of knowing the boundaries. They need to know what behaviour is acceptable. They need to know that throwing food, breaking toys, having a tantrum is not acceptable. It is vital for them to realize that it is the act which is frowned on, not them. Hearing parents say, 'I won't love you if you do that', stores up trouble for the future. It is important to avoid confrontations. 'I'm not going to school this morning', should be ignored and a conversation about breakfast, or the clothes to be worn will take the child's mind off the problem. Giving in to children for the sake of peace and quiet again is storing up trouble. They will expect you to give in on more and more issues.

In all of these areas children grow and develop as individuals. Nowadays, education in primary schools is not for the mass of children but for individual children. They are all different and need to be treated differently. When a class teacher is angry or shouts at a room full of children, some will worry a great deal and take notice, others will not be affected in any way, still others will feel resentful and angry that the teacher has spoken in such a way to them. It all depends on the individual. Parents who have more than one child have to recognize and accept the different behaviour and attitudes of their children. If the first one is able to walk at 12 months it does not necessarily mean that subsequent children will do the same. Similarly, one girl may be interested in music, another daughter may be interested in chess.

As our children grow older the situation changes. Once they have started school their lives are dominated by the happenings at school. A happy school life is of great importance in the way attitudes to learning are adopted.

Pre-school work, as previously stated, helps a child to learn informally. School gives another dimension to learning. It's an institution and as parents we expect our children to come home and tell us what they have learned. In the early (5 – 7) years it is relatively easy. We help them with their reading. We help them with their 'sums' and tables and spellings etc., but gradually, as they get older, we find that the maths problems are more difficult. The children seem to know and tend to look surprised when we irritably tell them we are too busy, we'll help them later, and then conveniently forget. This holds true of every subject and with many children. There comes a time when a question is asked which we as parents are unable to answer. How we handle that situation reflects our attitude to learning perhaps. If we feel threatened we can lose our temper and comment on the stupid subjects that are taught in schools today; or we can frankly admit we don't know (which takes courage). The important point is our calmness must be maintained. It is necessary to remain in control of the situation or as one child said to me, 'I won't ask you as I know you're no good at that subject'. That same child knew that there were some subjects which I was capable of giving help and others where support had to be sought elsewhere.

Teenagers are very difficult to have around the house. They are mixed up, growing up, fed up, and cheesed off. One minute the world is their oyster and the next it has come to an end. Coping with them takes patience and tact. Dr Faith Spicer claims they need the wall of parental support to bang against. They need to know exactly how far they can go before you explode. A teenager, Christopher, turned to his sister and said, 'It's OK Catherine, she's not shouting loud enough yet!!' He knew exactly the pitch when his mother would stand no more fooling. The wall of support is there for them to bang their heads against. It gives them security in an uncertain world. If we have built up a good relationship of shared confidences with our children when young, it should continue. There will be times when there will be a deliberate attempt to shock. A joke or an expression or the recounting of an incident will be used to measure the extent of your tolerance. A limit has to be placed but, as when they were much younger, it is the deed, not themselves, which offends.

Helping with the school work in the teenage years can be easy if it is a question in a subject with which you are familiar. If it is in an unfamiliar subject, it will be necessary to do some research. A wise father we know asks his son's teachers at the beginning of each school year for a written report of the work to be covered. If they are not too expensive, he buys some of the books; or, when he has time, he visits the local library. He is a dedicated father and not many of us can be so dedicated. Fortunately, most homes have telephones and when children receive a negative response from you, they can and should get into the habit of talking to their peers. They should also get into the habit of visiting their local libraries themselves. Teenagers are fortunate in the mid-1980s, so many television documentaries help them with history, geography, literature, science, medicine, etc. When most parents went to school they learned about glaciers from a text book. They learned about the Battle of Waterloo from a history book. Now teenagers can see all of these in glorious technicolour in their living rooms.

THE THREE Cs

Microorganisms can be readily seen on a TV screen with appropriate explanations given. With the explosion of information technology, we as parents should sit and learn with our teenagers. They will mainly take their attitude to the world from us. There will be a time when they will revolt and refuse to consider our knowledge as being of any use. The music we listen to is 'Fogey music'. Nevertheless, what we are, how we behave, how we accept them will affect how they feel about themselves, about us, and about other people. If we are tolerant of other people's attitudes and behaviour, if we show no prejudices, they will accept that people are different, not worse, just different. Our attitudes to crime and punishment will initially be theirs, as will our attitude to peace, nuclear weapons, birth control, etc. As parents we are the main educators of our children; even if they totally reject our beliefs, we will still have helped them form whatever beliefs they hold.

Parents should be delighted in the development of micro technology. It enables their children to learn at home, at their own pace, and allows them to follow their individual inclinations. As more and more software becomes available it will be possible to learn all the so-called basic skills using a micro. By basic skills we mean reading, writing, maths, science, geography, history, etc. In other words all the subjects normally associated with school work can be learned via a computer. Parents no doubt will be delighted; but obviously this does raise questions which need to be answered.

AS A PARENT, HOW DO I START?

For a parent the problem of getting started is not much different from that of a teacher wishing to get started. As we discussed before, begin by talking to friends, go to your local library, browse in bookstores and magazine racks, try to find a friendly computer buff, ask your children's teachers, look for courses offered for beginners, attend lectures, etc. But act! Your children's future is at stake.

The early part of this chapter concentrated on the educational environment that already exists at home. This should continue as children grow up to live in similar situations. Again the emphasis is on talk and conversation. Gradually in more and more homes micros will become part of that environment. Just as radio, then television, telephone, and videos have gradually become part of life, the same will hold true of a micro. In most families it is the teenagers who learn to use the video, hog the telephone, and walk around with a 'walkman' stuck in their ears. This will not hold true of the computer. The age of the computer whizz-kid will get younger. We read of fourteen- and fifteen-year-olds earning thousands of pounds by virtue of having written a popular game program for computers.

Parents need to know what makes a good computer program. This has been dealt with in an earlier chapter. In an ideal situation there will be many good programs covering all topics, starting with pre-language and maths programs.

Young toddlers will automatically want to touch the keys, use the light pen, draw pictures, as they do with any article in the house. Gradually they can be led on to early language and maths programs – programs which will make them talk, express opinions, and learn basic language and maths skills. Programs which allow a choice of options and alternative endings will greatly enhance the language. Likewise programs which present mathematical problems in an interesting and lively manner will encourage a positive attitude to solving more complex mathematical problems later.

The role of the parent in all of this has to be positive and cooperative. A very young child has a short concentration span and this must be taken into account. Just as the majority of teachers in schools adopt a flexible approach to the work to be done, so must a parent. For example, most teachers plan in advance the work they hope to do in a day, a week, a half-term etc. If the planning is too rigid, it does not allow for the unexpected happening, such as a child who brings a frog to school. A valuable learning experience could be missed. In the same way parents should loosely plan the kind of programs they want their child to work through, but if something more valuable turns up – a hot day invitation to the beach, or the first snow of winter – the choice is obvious.

If a daughter is forced to sit through a computer program just because dad wants her to learn decimals, or a son forced to learn French, the resentment caused will make it doubtful whether the information picked up will be stored in long-term memory. Drill and practice programs are boring and should be avoided unless they have been carefully selected to help reinforce a particular basic skill.

Problem-solving and simulation exercises can be great fun and a marvellous learning experience. Most of them, however, need at least one other person to work through the program. If there are other children in the family, or family friends, who can be encouraged to join in, so much the better. Working with a computer should be treated as a life-skill situation. Not only is a specific problem being solved (e.g. finding the pirates' treasure) but the children are learning to argue, work, discuss, and tolerate each other's point of view.

Eventually computers in homes will be linked to terminals around the world. Parents will be able to set problems for their children to solve. Instead of asking your child merely, 'What shall we have for tea?', it should also become possible to ask, 'Has the fruit shop put my order up yet and how much does it cost?' The answer will, of course, be displayed on the computer screen.

Children need time to be on their own. This does not mean locked in a room, glued to a computer. It means there are times when they need to solve their own problems, at their own pace. On every computer there is a delete button which rubs out mistakes. Children need to make mistakes. No matter how carefully we try to protect them, nothing teaches them better than their own experiences. If a child is allowed to work alone, the look of concentration and pleasure is a joy to behold. A child watching a butterfly or a kitten is enraptured. So it can be with computer programs. The excitement of winning and working through a program unaided is an experience a child will not forget easily. This will not happen if an adult is constantly interfering. A child can learn if left in front of a computer just as a child will learn if left alone to observe leaves and colours and birds and insects.

On the other hand a child also needs an appreciative audience. Winning a race, learning to swim are exhilarating experiences, but

140

they are enriched if Mum or Dad are there to encourage and praise. There are many things which children have to struggle to learn. Learning to knit is very difficult. Why, when ten stitches have been cast on, does a young child find at the end of a row that there are twenty stiches on the needle? A caring and appreciative adult will carefully and patiently teach a child to knit. A child cannot learn to knit alone. Knitting needs to be taught.

The most important thing a parent has to learn is the capabilities of their offspring. One will be independent and seem to need very little help, another will need a great deal of help and encouragement. It takes skill to be an able teacher or parent. Patience is the all-important ingredient. If a child is struggling with a program, put it away for another day. Instead, immediately find something that the child can do − something which builds confidence. Always give praise when praise is due.

Using a computer does not rule out all the equipment which is available for children. Story books are a joy and a house full of books is indeed a rich educational environment. Pencils, crayons, and paints to stimulate creativity − dolls, trains, balls, swings − all are valuable in a learning situation. Toys need to be carefully bought. Today's toys can so easily become tomorrow's rubbish. Toys which stimulate the imagination, e.g. train sets, or dolls are valuable. Toys which help manipulative control, e.g. jigsaws, balls, skipping ropes, are valuable. Lego and building bricks, dressing up clothes, sand and water are invaluable aids to learning.

Computer peripherals are becoming readily available. Light pens which draw pictures on the screen provide delight and satisfaction. Children feel as though they are writing on television. It's the same as seeing their name at the beginning of a program. It helps them to identify with their work or with the program. It is also a lot less messy.

Word processing is growing in importance. Children will have to learn how to write conventionally, even if it is just to pass notes to each other in class. The word processing facility has three distinct advantages over conventional writing:

(1) The letters are presented the right way round. How many times

do children become confused with b, d, p. On the word processor the letters are always correctly shown.

(2) Children have to be taught to read left to right. When using a word processor the writing always starts at the left-hand side in the correct way.

(3) Usually when children are just learning to write, the words are all joined together in one continuous line which usually slopes down or up the page. Using the word processing facility on the micro, produces lines which are straight. Furthermore, the letters are all the same size and, generally, the children do not forget to press the space bar which separates each word. This presents a neat and tidy piece of work. It can be argued that it destroys the individuality of writing. The individuality lies in the content of the work rather than the way the letters are formed. The most beautiful poetry is a joy to read, especially if it is easy to understand the writing.

Gradually more and more computer-based toys are coming into the homes. Big-Trak was one of the first. Children enjoy having control of the vehicle and rapidly learn how to send it off in various directions. Parents should be aware that this is a problem-solving exercise and requires skill and forward planning that no other toy has demanded. Train sets could be said to perform a similar function, but they are not as free-running and tend to be expensive. Gradually computer-based toys will become cheaper. Turtles came onto the market next. These are valuable in that they allow for experimentation and forward planning. They also encourage children's awareness of space − their own body space and the space of their immediate environment. The turtle unobtrusively helps mathematical concepts.

If your child is going to have the advantage of micro-technology at home there could be a situation where she has learned more than any conventional school could teach her. It depends on what parents expect from a school-based education. Generally speaking the teaching of the three Rs is still held to the *the* educational criterion. In that case, schools will have little to offer in the future. But gradually schools are moving away from this basis. In fact, since the abolition of the eleven-plus examination system, most primary schools in England have broadened their curriculum. This has led to a broad-based education involving all the developmental competencies. Many of these need to be shared with a peer group, e.g. cooperating, discussing, associating, creating, etc. The role of schools will have to change in keeping with computer development. If they do not, then many problems will be created. Children will be able to read, write, and do maths before they even start school. This makes it even more important for schools and families to work in partnership. Children's progress will be carefully monitored. Fortunately, as schools acquire more and more micros, most subjects will be taught by computer. What cannot be taught by computer are the interactions with other people with all their multiple reactions. Learning to cope with, handle, and help other people, developing physical skills, working through scientific projects, and caring for the environment will still need to be taught in schools with subjects perhaps not yet realized.

Most of this chapter has dealt with younger children. However, the principle holds for older children and teenagers, as well. Provide them with a stimulating and sympathetic environment. Just as you might buy them books, buy them education software. Set up neighbourhood cooperatives so that parents and youngsters can share software. The chances are that if you have teenagers, they are already into computers, at least into computer games. Ask them to help you. It will make them feel good to teach you something.

At the Ninth Australian Computer Conference in 1982, a father and daughter team presented a paper entitled 'The Computer in the Home' [2]. The father, Alan Brown, worked in the Operations Research Department of an insurance company. The daughter Fiona, attended a girls grammar school in the Melbourne area. Her view of having a computer in the home was that it: '... brought many changes to all of our family. The computer is now used for school assignments, games galore, homework for Dad, and as an all-purpose filing cabinet'. She went on to state that:

> For me the major benefit of our computer has been the doing of much of my schoolwork on it. Assignments especially are things that take a lot of time to organise, edit, and then present neatly and tidily. With a computer a lot of this

editing and organising is either eliminated or made a lot easier. The editing can be cut down because the one copy can be altered or rearranged without the need to be completely rewritten. Also you do not have to do the questions in order because you can sort them into the correct sequence later. On the other hand there is no way that you can rearrange ink on paper.

Fiona goes on to cite teacher reaction:

Such assignments certainly impressed my teachers with their neatness and easy readability. But I suspect that some people thought that the computer was a magical instrument that was asked questions and answered in beautiful paragraphs suitable for an assignment. These people really didn't believe that I did any work. 'Although this is extremely well presented, there is far too much straight copying and little of your own efforts other than a great ability to organise! C.' But thankfully there were not too many of these people and most of the teachers were impressed with the work I was able to produce. 'Quite amusing situations; told well and ends very well. Expression a bit stilted. Punctuation errors with full stops and commas: use more conjunctions. A.'

I was not the only one that did assignments on the computer. My younger brother also used the computer for most of his work. But this time we made sure that the teacher knew that it was his work by having her come for a demonstration one afternoon. This teacher was impressed by his knowledge of the computer and accepted all of his printed work gratefully as he is normally a messy worker. His efforts were very successful and much improved on previous work.'

If you didn't have a computer in your home or, alternatively, if you have one but don't know what to do with it, find neighbours, friends, acquaintances, enemies – anybody – to meet with one evening a week – like playing bridge, going out to a film, or watching home video films – and form a computer discussion group. Education, like charity, begins at home.

Many parents push their children. They put great pressure on them to advance rapidly in their education. The body of human knowledge has grown at such a pace that it becomes impossible for any child to learn everything. But then, this is not necessary. The sign of an educated person is not what they know – what specific bits of information they keep in their heads – it is the ability to obtain the information needed, when it is needed – and to understand it.

A computer in the home coupled to data bases and expert systems around the world, will not only provide an information-rich environment, it is probably the best way to teach children basic information skills.

Chapter 11
Advanced Language and Professional Skills (for Academics only)

That great pioneer of the computer revolution, Christopher Evans, in his book *The Mighty Micro* [1], devotes Chapter 8 to 'The death of the printed word'. Evans begins by stating that the 'invention of writing was the most revolutionary of all human inventions . . .'. Facts could remain as a permanent record after their originator had forgotten them or had passed away into dust. Ideas could move from one individual to another across time and space. 'The significance of permanent data storage is the principal and perhaps the *sole* reason why Man is so absolutely the dominant creature of the planet'. As Chris Evans points out, the book has been 'such a long-loved and useful companion to mankind that one should not speak lightly of its decline and ultimate disappearance'. Nevertheless, Evans concludes that there are a number of reasons why the decline is imminent: the computer is so vastly superior to the book, that it will displace it as a means of storing information.

The first parameter involves size. We are now able to store entire libraries in electronic devices the size of a single book. The second parameter concerns costs. We have already referred to examples such as the *Oxford English Dictionary*, which is putting itself into a computer. The overriding reason is the cost factor. The third factor is the versatility of the new medium: electronically, you can still, if you wish, print a book out into a standard format. But the books of the future will be hand-held VDUs with computers in them. The screen on which the text is displayed will vary in size depending on what one wants. For that hand-held book you would want it regular page size. For quick reference and portability, a wrist size might be sufficient. Most attractive is a ceiling projection for reading in bed – as Chris Evans says: 'At last!'

The books of the future will no longer be passive, regurgitating only the information stored in a fixed form. Instead, the 'smart' encyclopaedias of the future will do their own research, acting as a study partner for anyone who needs to have access to any complex pattern of information.

At the time Chris Evans was writing, the possibility of such a book had already been explored by Alan Kay, the originator of the Dynabook. Kay envisioned such a book in the late 1960s, when the technology still had another quarter of a century to go. He worked for the Xerox Learning Research Group and was able to design a special communications system. A prototype of the Dynabook concept was built, centred on a powerful programming language, 'Smalltalk'. The system was set up as a learning resource centre in a local junior secondary school. The system, though not portable, allowed students to use this 'interim Dynabook' as a file cabinet, an interactive memory, a word processor with several fonts, a device for painting, animating and composing music, or any combinations of these, for stimulating ... in short, almost all of the sorts of things we have discussed previously. Reviewing the possibilities of the Dynabook, Kay and Adele Goldberg [2] conclude that if '... such a machine were designed in a way that any owner could mold and channel its power to his own needs, then a new kind of medium would have been created: a metamedium, whose content would be a wide range of already-existing and not-yet-invented media'. Architects could view their drawings in three dimensions. Composers could hear their compositions while they were in progress. Artists could vary sketches at will, and scientists could simulate experiments.

Ultimately, the Dynabook would be the size and thickness of a standard writing pad, it would have a detachable keyboard, a photosensitive 'light-pen' to draw on the screen and it would have a good quality loudspeaker. In addition, it would have a plug-in memory pack, the size of a credit card, which could store the text and pictures of five average-sized books, or five minutes of synthesized speech.

THE THREE Cs

The features of such a book have been discussed more recently by Dr Mike Sharples of the Department of Artificial Intelligence at Edinburgh University [3]. Sharples considers using this device in a number of ways. First, it would be 'a window on knowledge'. It could be used as the intelligent encyclopaedia Chris Evans talked about. It would be able to access data bases and expert systems around the world. Sharples describes using his own computer, spending an absorbing night exploring ARPAnet, a communications network which links many of the academic computers in the USA. Among others, he describes a rather uncomfortable few minutes interacting with the 'Parry' program, which can converse in normal English language, but simulates a paranoiac. He found it rather spooky, and therefore shifted to the computer in California which collects the newswire reports sent out by the UPI Press Agency. The computer automatically files these news reports under topic headings, and Sharples was able to find out what was happening about nuclear power on the West coast, or all the news stories appearing in the US on Margaret Thatcher. Sharples spent the night leap-frogging from one computer to the next, reading research reports, looking at demonstration programs, and leaving messages for colleagues. It was the first time that he had entered a large network, and he was struck by the ease with which he could travel along the paths that connect computers, and by the immense store of knowledge he had glimpsed.

With a Dynabook, Sharples points out, news and information will no longer be a precious resource. It will be what appears on the screen after the junk mail and jargon have been filtered out. This places a great onus on the reader. 'Children of the computer age need to learn not only the skills of information retrieval, but also of discrimination and information rejection.'

Sharples envisions using the Dynabook not so much as an encyclopaedia-type text book, but as a 'non-linear' text book. He cites examples of moving through 'European geography', by branching into 'Western Europe' then the 'population' thereof, and moving around from one area to another, the way you might browse through an encyclopaedia, but of course, with much more information and much greater depth available than any printed encyclopaedia could possibly provide.

A Dynabook author is not restricted to a single stream of text. An author could create stories along the lines of 'Storymaker', a program developed by Andrew Rubin, which offers children a 'tree' of possible stories. It starts by displaying the first few sentences of a story on the screen, and suggests branches that continue the story. The child can move along various paths, from trunk to branches to twigs, and different paths mean different sets of stories with different endings. The final twig on the tree ends a story. Children who use 'Storymaker' found that their early choices had definite, sometimes surprising, consequences. By exploring different paths, they began to learn about the structure and coherence of stories. This is only the first step. A child can add personal branches to the 'Storymaker' tree by typing in alternative endings, or complete story segments. In the process, the child learns to read carefully and plan the writing, not as part of a dreary exercise, but as an act of creation. The Dynabook facilities would allow an author to create computer cartoons by drawing a few pictures, then commanding the computer to fill in the action. This is a technique which is already in use in large computers, which have such animation systems. As Sharples points out, add music and you have a computer *Fantasia*.

Because it is possible to communicate to others, one could envision groups of eleven-year-olds on several different continents cooperating to write a computer story which might, among others, include a video game.

COMPUTER POETRY

Dry path

Lonely moon fades subtly
In cold plains
Black clouds
Frost fades by wish

THE THREE Cs

We feed slowly

Black path fades to red rocks
I feed

This poem was written by a fifteen-year-old boy with the aid of a computer program written by Mike Sharples [4]. As Sharples points out, the purpose of the exercise was not to create an inspired work of art, but to give children the opportunity to explore their own language in a creative and engaging project: 'To most people, language is a nebulous substance. In everyday speech and writing we create patterns of words without being conscious of the linguistic conventions that bind them. Computer programs can make language more tangible, by providing data structures that represent linguistic rules, styles and conventions, and procedures that generate and accept text according to a given set of rules'.

We have discussed LOGO in a previous chapter in connection with Turtle Geometry. Sharples uses LOGO in a most ingenious way for teaching literacy skills. He devised a PUT command to create a box into which a number of words can be put. For example, a box called SHAPE may contain the words: 'square', 'triangle', and 'circle'. Whenever the command SHAPE appears as part of a super-command, the words 'square', 'triangle', or 'circle' may come up at random.

The above illustrates how a child may group words together into a class. It is only a small step from classifying shapes into classifying words according to parts of speech. By creating boxes for NOUNS, VERBS, ADJECTIVES, and other parts of speech, as well as special categories (e.g. NAMES), children can begin to modify existing stories. For example, the input (Command)

'Mr NAME is a very ADJECTIVE man'

becomes

'Mr Sprogs is a very hairy man'

Such a procedure can be extended to create the sentence:

ARTICLE ADJECTIVE NOUN VERB ARTICLE NOUN

150

If the four kinds of boxes contain the following nine words, as follows:

ARTICLE	a, the
NOUN	mouse, cat, lion
ADJECTIVE	big, tiny
VERB	eats, devours

then the computer might create the sentence:

'a tiny cat devours the mouse'

or

'a big lion eats the lion'

Sharples goes on to extend the original LOGO program to generate haiku, a simple form of poetry from ancient Japan. An example of a haiku is

Late cool showers fall.
Tiny blossoms open and
Greet the new warm sun.

The word pattern for this poem is:

ADJECTIVE ADJECTIVE NOUN VERB
ADJECTIVE NOUN VERB CONJUNCTION
VERB ARTICLE ADJECTIVE ADJECTIVE NOUN

Haiku is written about nature and its seasons. Sharples chooses:

ADJECTIVE	still, lifeless, fragile, white, hungry
NOUN	petal, bird, flower, snowflake, rock
VERB	stands, moves, falls, soars, waits, sings
CONJUNCTION	and, then
ARTICLE	a, the

151

THE THREE Cs

The computer might now generate:

> hungry lifeless bird falls
> white rock sings then
> waits a still still petal

There are further refinements possible. The output of one program can be fed into a second program which has pre-written rules to further transform and tidy up the grammar. Each provides further insight into how sentences are constructed.

Sharples considers that one of the joys of a complex non-deterministic program is its capacity to surprise. For example, he delighted in:

> Why does my waiting child like to talk?
> Why does my girl wish to dream of my song?
> You are like a song.
> By herself my waiting girl dreams.

As Sharples points out, a computer is no more a poet than a programmable calculator is a mathematician. Any imagination and sentiment in the poems comes from the programmer's choice of words and grammatical rules. Sharples' creation 'GRAM' is just one of a set of computer aids for language exploration and creative writing. The programs, which include a text transformer, an automated thesaurus, and a story planner, were incorporated in a computer-based teaching scheme for creative writing and tested with eleven-year-old children. The same programs have been used by university students to investigate linguistic structures. By building computer representations of language we, children and adults alike, can discover new patterns in languge.

We are excited by Sharples's work. It represents another example of enhancing human creativity by using the computer as a tool. We are also reminded of eight-year-old Emma's comment about her computer:

> I liked it because it did all the writing.
> All we did was the thinking.

152

LINGUISTICS AND ARTIFICIAL INTELLIGENCE –
CREATE YOUR OWN LANGUAGE

A character distribution analysis of Act III of *Hamlet* indicates that, aside from punctuation marks, there are a total of 35,224 characters including letters, spaces and apostrophes. Of these, about one-fifth (6,934) are spaces; there are 3,277 Es, 2,578 Os, 2,557 Ts, but only 34 Js, 27 Qs, 21 Xs, and 14 Zs. There are 203 apostrophes. William R. Bennett [5] examines the idea that if enough monkeys were allowed to pound away at typewriters for enough time, all the great works of literature would result. Bennett considers the astronomical volume of sheer rubbish that would be produced in the process. He cites the comedian, Bob Newhart, who imagined such an experiment, providing a staff of tireless inspectors to read all the typed material. After much unrecognizable and unpronounceable drivel – great excitement! A recognizable fragment has appeared: Inspector at Post 15 catches: 'to be or not to be ... that is the *gesornenplatz*'.

Bennett points out that the probability of even this one sentence appearing would require a good monkey typist, typing steadily at 10 characters per second, an average of 10^{36} years (i.e., a 10 with 36 zeros behind it) to accomplish.

To help the monkey out, Bennett utilizes a method based on the statistical properties of the English language. The first level of help would be to provide the monkey responsible for typing Act III with a specially constructed typewriter with 35,224 keys, each representing one of the characters used in Act III. Needless to say, rather than constructing such an elaborate typewriter, a computer can be programmed to pretend it has such a set of 35,224 keys.

A talented monkey would still type gibberish, but it would be broken down into word-length sequences since, on average, every fifth key represents a space between letters.

The second level involves correlating pairs of letters. The most obvious in the English language is that a Q is always followed by a U. One can make a statistical analysis of how frequently one letter is followed by another. In Act III, for example, the E is frequently followed by a space, indicating the high probability that a word will

153

end in E. Similarly, a space is frequently *followed* by a T, reflecting the higher probability of words beginning with T. Likewise, there are higher probabilities for T being followed by H, and by H followed by E (THE). There are 28 × 28 possible two-character combinations (total 784). In Act III, only 291 out of those possible 784 combinations appear, showing that English has a lot of rules about which letters follow which.

As we apply the restrictions involving the two-letter sequences, the monkeys' typed gibberish begins to look more like English gibberish than German or French − even more so if we analyse three-letter sequences. For example, QU is most likely to be followed by the letter E, I, or A, in that order. By the time we are busy with three-letter sequences we begin to come up with real words. For example, there is a high probability of having the sequence THE − producing the commonest word in the English language. Similarly, AND, BUT, FOR WIT and YOU would, as Bennett puts it 'stand out like beacons in the night and will attract our third-order monkeys much as they would a bunch of moths'.

In fact, third level monkey output is beginning to look not merely like English (rather than French) gibberish, but it is beginning to look like Shakespeare (rather than Edgar Allen Poe) gibberish. Poe liked to use big words with lots of different letter combinations. Shakespeare, on the other hand, preferred more direct, concise statements useful for dialogue in a play.

A third level analysis considers 28 × 28 × 28 possible character combinations, totalling about 22,000 possibilities. This begins to stretch computer memories. Bennett reports that the yield of real words from the fourth-order Shakespeare monkeys was roughly 90 per cent. Furthermore, strong style-dependent differences were detected between different authors. Fourth-order monkeys also create differences between languages which are sufficiently pronounced to fool someone not familiar with the language. For example, a fourth-order medieval Latin monkey text based on statistics computed from Roger Bacon's thirteenth-century writings seems about as real as the original source of text.

Bennett attached his computer to a voice chip. As with letter-character sequences, one can set up a matrix analysis for spoken phoneme sequences. A third-order phoneme matrix based on Hamlet's Act III produced, among others: 'LORD HAVE THEE DISH'D MOTHER. OPHELIA IS RANCID!' By fourth-order, almost all the groups of letters were words. There is no theoretical reason why more powerful computers might not carry out fifth order, or even higher, character sequence analyses. Bennett asks, how far need one go before the computer presents an interesting new thought or idea?

Bennett postulates that most educated people have some version of a third-order letter-correlation matrix in their heads, with rules, such as 'I before E except after C'. He wonders whether the human brain in learning spelling does anything very much different from the processes described above. He ponders further: 'Does anyone really doubt that a monkey program using fourth- or fifth-order correlation matrices loaded with clichés would be indistinguishable from the average political speech?'

The educational importance of using the computer to dissect words into letter patterns and analyse spelling is three-fold. First, and most obvious, it provides insight into language. The concept that third-order monkey gibberish may sound like English, French, or Latin gibberish, depending on the frequencies of certain letter combinations, is itself interesting. Analysing the patterns of a William Shakespeare, an Edgar Allan Poe, or an Ernest Hemingway, creates insights not attainable in other ways. We would suggest changing other parameters as well – for example, altering the ratio of consonants to vowels to produce Slavic-sounding (a lot of consonants) or Polynesian-sounding (a lot of vowels) languages. As far as we are aware, such programs do not exist as yet for classroom use – both hardware and software technology will have to progress further. However, they will come. When they do, pupils using computers, can play with language at the letter level, as we now play with language at the word level, using crossword puzzles.

It is the element of play which is so important. The computer, by presenting us with such a huge number of possibilities and combinations, allows the unexpected to happen. Sooner or later, it surprises us. It also represents a challenge: how to make it produce the language or poetry we want. Because it is open-ended, this is computing at its best. It becomes addictive.

By working with a computer in this manner, we not only learn about languages, we also learn about statistics and computers. It is a way of bridging the gap between the culture of letters, and the culture of numbers.

The third significant learning experience relates to our brain and how it functions. Instructing the computer to arrange sequences to create words, as in Bennett's work, or words to create sentences or poetry, as in Sharples's work, makes us wonder how a brain functions. The bulk of our abstract thinking is accomplished by manipulating that system of symbols which we call language. To play with a computer, instructing it to create new languages gives us models about manipulating abstract symbols. At some point, as Bennett has said, you begin to wonder whether the computer is thinking. And the moment you begin to wonder about the computer thinking, you begin to wonder about thinking itself. The mental dialogue between you and artificial intelligence has begun.

The above technique has practical applications as well. It has obvious applications for cryptography. In addition, the technique has been used for identifying 'ghost writing'. For example, if there is a dispute about the authorship of some piece of work by Jane Austen, or Lewis Carroll, a statistical analysis of letter combinations or word frequencies would provide evidence one way or another.

LET THE COMPUTER CORRECT THE SPELLING

Not unrelated to an analysis of the sequence of letters, is an analysis of common spelling errors. The work of Yannakoudakis and Fawthrop [6] provides such a program. These workers analysed 1,377 types of spelling errors collected from existing literature and from poorly spelled text produced by adults. They found that the vast majority of spelling errors followed specific rules. These rules are based on phonological (sound) considerations, or relate to letter sequencing. Utilizing these rules they created an 'intelligent spelling error correction system' [7] to be used in a word processor. The system contains within it a standard dictionary of 93,769 words. Providing the intended word is in the dictionary, the computer is able to identify 80–90 per cent of the spelling errors.

This is an intelligent word processor system. It is, of course, an idiot savant with no knowledge of context or semantic structure. However, it does have information of possible pronounciations, and it also knows about the kind of spelling mistakes adults are likely to make. It knows which portion of the dictionary is likely to include the word in question. If a word is mis-spelled it invokes a number of tests and considerations (provided by Yannakoudakis and Fawthrop). As these authors describe it, when the system tries to correct the word AB-LITY, it rapidly abandons its examination of the word ANNUAL because of the large difference (five characters) between these two words. Similarly, when it tries to correct ALOW, it gives a much higher probability to ALLOW than to AGLOW.

Clearly, these sytems are still beyond the microcomputer systems of the mid-1980s. However, the hardware will improve, and so will our understanding of mis-spelled words. Probably a smaller dictionary with still more sophisticated spelling algorithms will allow a correction rate of 95 per cent or better, using personal microcomputers.

FIFTH GENERATION COMPUTERS

There has been much discussion about artificial intelligence and the fifth generation computers to which the Japanese have committed themselves as a national goal. It has been frequently assumed that these powerful fifth generation computers are to be big mainframe types. Not so. When Kazuhiro Fuchi, director of Japan's Institute for New Generation Computer Technology, was interviewed by David Ahl, editor of *Creative Computing* [8], he stated flatly: 'The real impact will be on the computers that are readily available to people – personal computers – rather than mainframes or supercomputers'. The technical ambition of the fifth generation project,

157

is breathtaking: to be able, by 1992, to build machines capable of one hundred million to one thousand million logical inferences per second – about ten thousand times faster than those in the early 1980s when the project was first begun [9].

Normally, given the general rate of progress, one would expect such an advance to occur over a twenty-year, rather than a ten-year period. However, these are dramatic times. Motorola, in the USA, announced [10] the MC 68020 chip in the summer of 1984, capable of 2.5 million operations per second. Although expensive, at $370 one must remember that its predecessor, the MC 68000 started at $250 in 1979, but had dropped to $35 five years later. The newer MC 68020 chip is 3/8 inch square and contains no less than 200,000 transistors spaced only two thousandth's of a millimetre apart. What the Japanese programme hopes to accomplish is to move computers from being mere information processors to advanced knowledge processors.

EXPERT SYSTEMS

Expert systems are intelligent data bases which do not merely regurgitate information, but which can actually provide professional advice. For example, expert systems will become increasingly important as an intellectual tool for doctors and pharmacists, both for diagnostic and for treatment purposes. Computer-assisted patient interviewing, whereby the computer utilizes expert systems, both to interrogate the patient and to analyse the findings, are beginning to move from the experimental stage to a more widespread application.

In computer-assisted patient interviewing, either the computer is used to interview the patient *before* the doctor talks to the patient – in which case the patient works with the computer directly – or, alternatively, the patient is interviewed by the doctor who is using the computer, as if it were an intelligent note pad.

One of the earliest medical programs involved diseases of the chest. The computer would ask questions which the patient would answer in private. Upon completion of the computer interview (about 20–30 minutes), the computer would then make the information provided by the patient available to the physician. The computer would point out the highly significant answers to the physician. For example, the question: 'Do you suffer from allergies?' might elicit the significant response: 'Yes', or, alternatively, the insignificant response: 'No'. In fact, the 'No' answer could be significant under certain circumstances, but only after the doctor had gained a clinical impression from the more significant answers. It would be up to the physician to interpret the facts.

Actually, the computer, because it contains an expert system, does more than merely play back the information provided by the patient. It not only organizes the information (as would befit an intelligent data base), it also compares the symptoms with sets of similar symptoms placed in its memory by one, or a team of expert consultants. In principle, this is no different from Yannakoudakis's system described above for comparing the spelling of a word with the spelling of similar words contained as a dictionary within the memory of the computer. The comparison of the patient's symptoms with a store of symptoms in the expert system, now allows the computer to draw certain inferences. The computer does not provide the physician with a firm diagnosis; rather it will suggest possibilities: 'Pleurisy 28 per cent, Tuberculosis 18 per cent, Lung Cancer 9 per cent etc.'. It may also suggest further diagnostic steps such as X-rays or blood tests.

The results of further diagnostic tests can then also be keyed into the computer. This would revise the probable diagnoses of the various pathologies: the expert system might now conclude that the probability of tuberculosis was up to 92 per cent. The computer, using a second expert system may also suggest various remedies. Given the multiplicity of drugs, the contra-indications, and the drug interactions, this could become a most valuable aid to physicians and pharmacists alike.

Such an expert consultations system, MYCIN, was developed at Stanford University during the 1970s. MYCIN was designed to assist doctors in selecting the right antibiotic, or combination of antibiotics for patients with serious infections. The knowledge contained within the system, and the rules for accessing this knowledge by the doctor using the system, was acquired from collaborating clinical experts during detailed discussions of specific complex cases on the wards at Stanford Medical Center in California. The system was also designed so that its knowledge could be increased through further interactions with other clinical experts. By the early 1980s MYCIN contained 700 rules dealing with the diagnosis and treatment of bacteremia (bacteria in the blood) and meningitis (bacteria in the cerebrospinal fluid). In addition, MYCIN may not only aid in diagnosing the problem, and suggesting an optimum treatment, it may admonish the physician to administer two antibiotics in separate IV (intra-venous) bottles: 'Since high concentrations of penicillins can inactivate amino-glycosides, do not mix these two antibiotics in the same IV bottle'. [11]

There are several problems associated with such systems: first, the reliability of the information put into the system; second, the appropriateness of the logical connections made between various types of information − that is the artificial intelligence being applied to the system; third, the relationship between the user (either the patient, or the doctor) and the expert system.

For example, when the chest program was first tried out on a number of patients, everything seemed to be going well until their first female patient. She seemed to be doing fine. As with other patients, she really became involved with the computer. Then, the shock − the stupid computer was asking her about her pipe-smoking habits!

A good program, properly field tested, avoids these problems. Almost all patients actually prefer the privacy of being interviewed by computer, knowing they will see the doctor later. Patients are also a lot more candid, revealing intimate aspects of their sex life, of problems with drink or drugs, much more readily to the apparently neutral computer than to a human interviewer. In a Glasgow hospital, patients interviewed by a computer admitted to drinking 42 per cent more alcohol than they did when interviewed by the clinic's highly trained consultants [12]. Similarly, Chris Evans who worked with Dr Hugh Price and others on the chest program, stated that patients visiting psycho-sexual clinics chatted eagerly to a computer about their private hang-ups whilst showing great reluctance to talk to the most sympathetic resident psychiatrists [13].

Knowing how to use the computer is important. Where the computer is used by the physician *during* the interview there is the problem of divided attention. This is particularly bad if it takes the computer ten seconds to respond to something the physician had keyed in. Ten seconds dead time is hell on an anxious patient. Whereas, in general, the experience of doctors using computers during the consultation was a favourable one, patients for whom the visit to the doctor was stressful did *not* welcome computers into the consultation [14].

More serious is the fact that expert systems are the product of Artificial Intelligence – a young field still grappling with basic problems such as knowledge representation, symbolic reasoning, natural language processing, speech understanding, methods of inference, program verification, decision analysis, and pattern recognition, to name but a few [15].

Against this, however, we must consider the rapid developments in the hardware, in artificial intelligence, and in medical practice. Future computer consultations will use videodisk systems with a patient's own physician or consultant asking questions from the screen, while the patient responds by talking to the computer, or using a finger to point to parts of the body displayed on the screen. These systems will become particularly important for people in Third World countries or in remote locations, because expert systems can be consulted at great distances – half-way around the world, if need be. Furthermore, as holographic techniques become better and cheaper, it will become possible to transmit three-dimensional images which would allow not only increasingly accurate 'tele-diagnosing', but also 'tele-surgery'. Where there is a shortage of qualified medical personnel, such facilities will obviously become a great help.

There is one other aspect of medical expert sytems which is important for educators to consider. It is said that a young, inexperienced, hospital registrar, upon being confronted by a new patient, makes a correct initial diagnosis only about 50 per cent of the time. A senior, experienced consultant will be up in the low 90s. A good expert system, relying on the computer alone, approximates the accuracy of the young registrar. Together, registrar plus computer will, after a short while, achieve a rate of correct diagnoses which begins to approach that of the senior consultant. When you take the computer away from the registrar, his or her accuracy drops – to, perhaps 70 per cent – but not to the original 50 per cent.

In other words, working with a computer can be an important learning experience for the registrar. For example, with the MYCIN system described above, the system may ask a question which the physician finds puzzling or irrelevant. When this occurs, the physician, instead of answering the question, responds with a WHY. MYCIN then indicates the reasoning behind its question. The physician may respond with further WHYs, or return to answering the original question. Even experienced consultants can learn from the combined knowledge of their colleagues stored in the expert system.

What is true for the medical profession is equally true for all other professions. Expert systems will invade law, accountancy, finance, architecture, etc. – even the education profession itself. By the mid-1980s, we had become used to automatic teller machines. But automatic bank managers? However, the banking industry is developing prototype computerized financial experts. Many decisions on whether to grant a loan are no different in principle from medical decisions based on the diagnostic systems described above. The only difference is that the bank manager is concerned with the client's financial, rather than physical health. Expert systems can help at more senior, company policy, decision-making levels as well. Security Pacific Bank in California is reported [16] to be developing a program that will predict foreign exchange rates. One of the main problems is for senior management to delegate decision-making to their juniors working with expert systems. It is this type of psychologial threat which will impede the rapid acceptance of expert systems (even when they are clearly advantageous).

Increasingly, expert systems will become available to the ordinary citizen as well. Some people still feel awkward about consulting a machine. However, they have no qualms about consulting their watch, or a thermometer. They have learned to trust the accuracy of their watches and thermometers.

Therein lies the danger! Expert systems deal with matters much more complex than the hour of the day or the temperature in the shade. They are therefore likely to be much less accurate. One of the functions of computer education must be to teach children, and adults, not to rely wholly on the answers and judgements of a machine. 'The computer says ...' should not be used as a final argument stating the correctness of any proposition. Unfortunately, the uneducated majority is always ready to believe the veracity of a proposition because they read it in a book or in their daily paper, or saw it on television. Computer-based information will add further verisimilitude to cherished beliefs and prejudices. On the other hand, the enlightened use of expert systems will be a great boon to the development and application of knowledge to human welfare. It represents the beginning of a communal brain which does more than merely remember and regurgitate information.

SOME PERSONAL EXPERIENCE WITH, AND THOUGHTS ON, INTELLIGENT DATA BASES AND ELECTRONIC PUBLISHING

It has been said that the last time it was possible to read all the books published in Europe was early in the Renaissance. Certainly it becomes practically impossible in the late twentieth century. However, the rapid increase in the number of electronic data bases and on-line systems, makes the problem more manageable. One of us (TS) has subscribed for many years to the Automatic Subject Citation Alert (ASCA) published by the Institute for Scientific Information (ISI) in Philadelphia. The Citation Alert works as follows.

The titles, authors, and references cited by a scientific paper published almost anywhere in the world are fed into a central computer. As a subscriber, I ask the computer to look out for one of several categories of information of interest to me. First of all, I ask for certain key words, key phrases, or combinations of words appearing in the paper's title. It need not be a complete word, but merely the stem or root. For example, 'Oxid' would include 'Oxidation', 'Oxidase', 'Oxide', 'Peroxide', 'Peroxidase', 'Peroxidation', 'Epoxide', etc. It would be a very foolish choice to ask the system

163

for 'Oxid' – it would yield references to hundreds, if not thousands, of papers each week. Similarly, 'Phenol' would yield 'Phenols', 'Phenolic', 'Phenolase', 'Diphenol', etc., and each week there would be hundreds of items containing 'Phenol' in their title. However, if I instructed the system to provide me with a title only if *both* 'Oxid' and 'Phenol' appeared, then the number of titles each week is reduced to a relatively small number.

A second approach is to ask the system to alert me to any articles published by a particular author, or, even more valuable, to instances when such a key author is cited in the list of references at the back of the paper. For example, I have included my own name on the theory that any worker who cites me is conducting research of interest to me. The Citation Alert covers hundreds of thousands of items each week. These will include the reports of the Bulgarian Academy of Sciences as well as of the US National Academy. ASCA covers some of the most obscure specialist journals as well.

Once a paper or article of interest has been identified it is possible to obtain the complete paper from ASCA. Alternatively, I may send a request for a reprint from the author (whose address is also listed on the weekly sheet), or go to the library. Incidentally, the title of an article appears on the weekly computer print-out sheet long before it appears in the library. The computer collects the information as the periodical goes to press. The library gets it only after it has come off the press, has been bound and mailed (often half-way around the world), and processed by the library. There will come a time in the future when I won't bother going to the library, or writing to the author for a reprint. I'll simply have my desk top, personal computer retrieve the entire article from the main computer. First, I may scan it on the screen, then decide whether I want a 'hard' copy by having the computer print out the paper, to take on my next train journey or to read in a more comfortable environment. In fact, I hate reading things on a screen. Present-day VDUs can produce eye strain, and constitute one of the least satisfactory aspects of the technology.

It may also be, in the future, that I do not submit a typed manuscript reporting my latest research findings to a journal; rather I let my computer/word processor send it electronically. The reviewer would not only get my manuscript, but would also have the computer call up articles with similar titles, and would be able to look at some of my cited references. He would then recommend whether the paper was to be published or not. If it was it would be entered into the appropriate data base, and all subscribers who had keyed in the appropriate instructions (such as key words and phrases) would be notified of the appearance of the new article. Note that this would be done instantly, not at the end of the month. Note also that nowhere in the process do printing presses appear – in fact, one does not even *have* to have paper in this process. This is what is meant by electronic publishing.

The Automatic Subject Citation Alert covers a wider and wider area of knowledge each year. I am now picking up not only references to work in the natural sciences but also, increasingly work in the social sciences. In due course, all fields of scholarly activity will be covered.

It is an unfortunate fact that pressures on academics all over the world to 'publish or perish' has caused an overload of publications. In many instances quantity exceeds quality. This may change in time as scholars publish via electronic data bases. We have cited above some applications of artificial intelligence to literature: letter sequence analysis, mis-spelling, and grammatical context. Work is going on to try to understand the intellectual content of paragraphs. The time may come when the intelligent data base itself may provide a commentary on any submitted paper before presenting it to a human reviewer. The data base may say: 'This paper supports the findings of Smith 1972 but is contrary to the conclusions of Jones 1984'. Or it may state very succinctly: 'This paper appears to be almost identical to the one you published two years ago'. Ah well!

The above relates to the rarefied atmosphere of upper academia. On the ground, electronic magazines and newspapers will appear in homes and offices. Writers, reporters, businessmen, and politicians will have at their fingertips vast sources of information. I know of one man, a pharmacist, who has decided to write a book on the lack of efficacy, and frequent abuse, of many drugs. He is using his home computer (with a modem) to access not only professional data bases dealing with drugs but also the 'Knowledge Index', a general encyclopaedic data base available to North American subscribers.

Once upon a time only monks and scribes used to know how to write letters and words. Now, practically everybody does. Today, only a few people know enough to write books. In the future, with expert systems to provide information, and word processing to correct the spelling and grammar, practically anybody will be able to write a book. For better or worse, we have moved into an information age.

Section IV
Towards the future

Chapter 12
Interlude in the Year 2010

The warm spring breeze blew through the windows as the Hobart family began to start the day. Grandad, who never slept for long, had already completed his exercises. He had used his wrist computer so no-one had been disturbed by the music and instructions transmitted to his earpiece as he exercised in the garden. Grandad felt better. The special exercises which had been programmed into his computer had increased his pulse rate to 115 for a few minutes, which was exactly what the doctor had prescribed as part of his Preventive Medicine Program.

He wandered through the kitchen and into the baby's bedroom. Wendy, at 8 months, was gurgling in her cot, watching the play of light patterns on the ceiling. The colours and shapes varied in accordance with the baby's sound pattern. As she called out, the patterns changed more abruptly, but nothing strong enough to suggest she was uncomfortable. The computer quite rightly indicated that, for the time being, she was content. Grandad bent down and kissed her and went through to take his shower.

The peace was shattered as Jill and John came down the stairs arguing. 'I think you're even more stupid than usual,' she yelled. 'The Beatles were bad enough with their drums and guitars, but you are making them a hundred times worse. Leave Mike (her pet name for the computer) on his own and even he could produce better music than you could dream of in a million years.' John pulled her back and shouted, 'Oh, so you're so clever you can do better than me, can you? That's rich, a skinny little 8-year-old thinks she is cleverer than a brother twice her age.' He held his computer closer to her ear so that the music was even louder than before. Jill struggled to free herself and shouted through the music, 'Get away from me – that stuff is rubbish!'

The noise they made disturbed Wendy, who began to cry, causing the bleeper in her parent's bedroom to wake them up. Dad jumped out of bed and ran down the stairs. Jill and John were still so angry they did not notice until their father yanked them apart, pushed them out into the garden and said, 'Stop that racket and get out there and do your workouts. We've had a bad night with Wendy teething and the last thing I want is you two yelling at this hour of the morning.' Sulkily, but not daring to disobey, John and Jill went out into the garden. They went to opposite ends, and using their personal workout programs, began to exercise.

The baby's distress had also alerted the household robot, who prepared the baby's bath and was in the process of preparing the breakfast for everyone. Dad went through to Wendy's room and picked her up, cuddling her, then tossing her in the air. He took her through into the bathroom and for the next 15 minutes, Wendy had a great time frustrating Dad's attempts to get her washed and dressed.

When Wendy was almost ready Graham sent a signal through to his wife's bedroom that they would be coming down for breakfast soon. Breakfast, although not a big meal, was an important one. Among other things, the family gathered to check with the computer and discuss the day's plans. The computer was used as a diary to remind them of the day's events and appointments, tell them whether they would need to use the car (and how to use it most efficiently), remind them of their favourite radio and TV shows (or tape such shows for future use), remind them when to meet for dinner (then instruct the automated kitchen to have dinner ready at that time), and, of course, deliver any electronic mail which might have arrived during the night, as well as the morning's custom-tailored newspaper.

Clare sleepily came to join Graham and the baby at the breakfast table. 'Every time these two meet it's the same thing', she grumbled. 'They would disagree on the colour of the sky, given half the chance.' She walked over to the computer and pressed her name key. The screen went blank apart from showing her name and the date at the top of the screen. Obviously she had no appointments for that day. She remained for two minutes staring at the blank screen, unable to make up her mind what to tell the computer about her plans for the day. 'I need something to eat first, then I'll decide', she said, and walked away back to the table and sat down. As she nursed her coffee, the others drifted in and joined her.

While they were eating there was very little conversation. Clare fed the baby, talking to her while turning over at the back of her mind the lecture she was producing. It still needed polishing. As the weeks passed the project had had some hiccups, but thanks to John's help with the background music and with his archive research the whole thing was beginning to come together. Her thoughts were interrupted when Wendy grabbed the spoon out of her hand, splashing milk and cereal all over. She scolded the baby and cleaned up the mess. Clare handed the baby to her mother-in-law and said, 'We need to decide what we will have for dinner tomorrow night. I want to wait until I can contact the Five Continents Foods manager personally. Last time I left the list on their computer, the curries they sent were Vindaloo instead of mild. This time I want to make sure that we get what *we* want for dinner not what they decide to give us!'

Tim leaned over shyly to speak to his Dad. At 12 years old, his 6 months visit to Pakistan was worrying him. He needed to sort things out so he could concentrate on his group's 'South East Asian Presentation' at school that afternoon. There were still a lot of loose ends to tidy up. 'Dad, have you found out our satellite time yet? If we're not careful it will all get booked up and I won't be able to talk to you while I'm away.' He had spent time in other parts of England, but that had not worried him. Through Anglonet computer phone he had been able to keep in daily contact with his family. Mum was always fussing and worrying unnecessarily, while Dad kept to the basics, like last time he was away and he needed new trainers. Through the computer Dad had found a sports shop in the Lake District where he could pick up the new ones. Dad just instructed the bank's computer teller to transfer the cash to the shop's account. 'Don't worry son, it's all arranged. We'll be able to see each other every three days just before you go to bed. Have you prepared your work for this afternoon, you were uptight about it on Sunday?' A grin spread over Tim's face. 'You bet Dad,' he said. 'Gran's "find" is going to help us win the competition.' He smiled at his Gran. 'Oh, how did she do that?', asked his Dad. 'Not telling. You will have to wait to see the recording tonight on the video.' He grinned happily.

'For goodness sake, can we get a move on?' snapped John. 'I've stacks of work to get through today and you lot just sit there waffling.' 'John!' warned his father. 'You've already been in trouble this morning and it's only 8.30 now, so I'd tread warily if I were you.' 'Sorry Dad,' answered John, 'I just want to get on. Can I put my timetable into the computer?' 'OK, go ahead,' replied Dad, 'but remember to check our timetables before you go to school this afternoon. With a menagerie like ours, even the best-running robots have difficulty coping, never mind us poor mortals. In any case, I want to speak to your teacher this afternoon, so don't forget to arrange that.' John walked over to the computer and began to dictate in his program, putting several queries where he wanted the freedom to change his mind.

'Trust you to get in first again,' said Jill with irritation, 'why can't I put my timetable in first for a change. You're always first and I have just as many things to do this morning as you.' 'Stop it Jill,' said her father. 'It only takes a minute and you can put yours in next.' After John and Jill left, Graham turned to his wife: 'Clare, I think you and I will need to look through some of those child psychology programs again. I don't know why these two argue all the time. There must be some useful advice the programs can give us.' Clare agreed and made a mental note to work through the psychology questionnaire on sibling relationships that evening. If necessary, she could consult the psychology expert system further. If that proved inadequate, she could use Euronet to contact the local psychologist. Perhaps it was just a phase they were going through. In any case, the software would ask the kinds of questions which would help towards such decisions.

Mrs Hobart and Clare wandered into the living room unaware that 4-year-old Andrew was following them. They were thinking of inviting their neighbours over for dinner the next day. During the conversation that ensued Andrew found out some interesting facts that could be of use to him later. He wondered why Janice was so fat and wore make-up that was blotchy. He also decided that when the Armstrongs came over the next night he would check to see whether Hal wore a wig; in fact, he would ask him whether it was a wig or if his hair was dyed.

Pondering on these matters he failed to notice Gran's attention had been drawn to him. 'Come on young man, time for you to get down to work. The others should be off the main computer by now and you need to do better than yesterday. Fancy making so many mistakes.' Andrew pulled a face and tried to struggle free, but in spite of her age, Grandma's strength prevented his escape. He liked the games on the computer, but he found some of the reading programs a bore. He did not want to know whether he had to climb the ladder to find the treasure or dig a hole in the field. However, Andrew knew better than to argue with his Gran and quietly he followed her into the living room and plonked himself down in front of his computer. He waited while Gran put in the cartridge, thinking all the while, 'I wish she'd let me do that. It's so easy. I'm a big boy now. Gran should look after Wendy, not me.' But Gran stayed with him and, in spite of himself, Andrew gradually became deeply involved in the story which, because it was on the micro, was different every day. As it unfolded on the screen the story became more and more exciting. Gran helped him with the words he couldn't understand. He liked to alter the story line, but then when he read it out loud, if often didn't make sense. Still, sometimes it came out funny. Other times it made Gran rather cross.

Graham finished typing his day's program into the computer and went to change the baby's program. Wendy had shown by her responses yesterday that she was thoroughly enjoying altering the colours and shapes which appeared on the walls and ceiling of her room. Graham decided he would include a more voice-sensitive response. The harder consonant sounds would form squares and rectangles of harsher colours, while the softer sounds would produce circles and semi-circles in delicate tones. He also felt that Wendy needed greater physical stimulus. The baby was increasingly more mobile in her playpen so he had programmed the robot Turtle toy to move around the outside of the playpen to encourage Wendy to move after it. Now, with the new program, she would discover that she could stop and start the turtle by making different kinds of sound.

When Graham finished with Wendy's program he ruminated on the information Tim had given him the night before on Pakistan. He decided to recheck the satellite time, as Tim might well be homesick and anxious to keep in constant touch. Six months away from home was a long time for a 12-year-old boy, but he would consolidate what he had learned about the people, language, and culture, etc. of Pakistan. He would be able to speak Urdu without a Yorkshire accent.

Clare and John had retired to the video room. Her lecture on Communication Skills needed to be completed as soon as possible. John, bless him, had helped with the research in communication in the 1960s. The fact that he was now involved with the Beatles was a bonus and the music he was producing would enhance the atmosphere of her presentation. She was amazed how primitive communication had been in the 1960s. The video films were so poor she had had to hire actors, scour museums and antique shops for telephones and TVs. Still, the scene they had re-enacted of the 1960s had been put together and it looked good. Trying to reach 40 million people was no mean feat, but at £20,000 a year for producing just one presentation per year, she was not about to complain. At least everyone watching was given the program in the language of their choice. She knew that John would be given good grades for his updating of the Beatles' music. She hummed some of the tunes as she continued working.

Jill was still angry with John and avoided him as she made her way to her Grandfather's room. The work she was doing with her doll's house was not going well and she needed Grandfather's help. Somewhere, somehow the current was faulty. There was perhaps some incompatibility between the light switches and the heating switches. She put the 'Doll's House' computing program on her Grandfather's computer, knowing quite well that he would come and help her. She put a Tommy Dorsey tape on, knowing that would attract his attention. She had grown to love the 'Big Band Sound' through Grandad. Later, when she had sorted out the house problem, she would put on the video of Tommy Dorsey, block out the pianist's playing, and play the piano herself. She adored Tommy Dorsey's *Boogie Woogie* even though she hadn't mastered it yet on the piano. 'If Grandad thinks my playing is good enough I'll tape it to fit Tommy Dorsey's orchestra.' Jill was looking forward to this afternoon at school. She had a swimming lesson. Her ambition was to be chosen for the school's synchronized swimming team, so she spent at least an hour a day practising various styles in the water.

Grandma was angry, the manager of the store had refused to come to the screen to assure her that the salmon for dinner the next day would be from Scotland and not imported. She was not a fussy person, but at her age she felt she was entitled to be a bit choosy. After all, she had been born in Scotland and it gave her happy memories to think about the Highlands. She would search the computer's yellow pages to find a more helpful supplier. As she skimmed through the stores on the screen she came across Tour Operators. Idly she called one up in Scotland. The word 'Trossachs' caught her eye. 'Why not? After all, they were retired, weren't they?', she thought to herself. She accidentally-on-purpose touched the key which automatically linked her with the screen of her husband's computer. Glancing out of the window she assured herself that Andrew was now enjoying playing outside in the garden with his friends. Looking again at the screen it showed she was linked to her husband's screen. Mischievously, she showed him the video of the Trossachs. The haunting Highland music really stirred her memories. Her husband appeared at the door. 'What are you doing woman?' He glowered, but she was not deceived. The twinkle in his eye gave him away. 'Well, it's spring, and I just thought of our first home. What about having a holiday there? Look, we could leave on Saturday and be away for as long or as short a time as you would like. You know we didn't take full advantage of the pensioners' holiday scheme last year.' 'All right, book it up,' he said. 'No wonder your son is a good Tour Organiser, he knows how to handle people. Just like you. I'm away to finish helping Jill. It's nearly time for school and we have finally sorted out the problem of the doll's house.'

This was true. Jill, now, was happily engaged in running her house. Her hands flew over the keys, opening doors, closing curtains, switching the heat off and on. Having completed the computer simulations of her house on the screen, she checked out the system in her real doll's house. She did this by moving her favourite doll from room to room. Satisfied, she kissed the doll and put it down on the couch. She knew that tomorrow's task was more difficult. She had to work out geographically where she wanted her house siting. Looking through weather maps, population distribution, towns and leisure facilities, etc. as shown on her computer, she had to decide where she would want to live if she was a working adult. Jill loved to excel. Her end-of-term report just had to be good!

No-one bothered with lunch except Wendy; the rest of the family just snacked at random. This meant that they all really looked forward to the evening meal.

Graham Hobart sat musing in front of his computer. Becoming an accountant had seemed like such a good idea back in the 1980s. In retrospect, the writing had been on the wall. Already by 1984, small businesses could buy, for substantially less than two-months' wages, software systems to run with their Apple microcomputers which would do the accounting, financial reporting, forecasting, job costing, stock control, modelling, and pay roll. This cheap system could handle up to a thousand accounts [1]. By the 1990s, not only small businesses, but virtually all professionals, retailers, home owners – in short the hundreds of thousands of small customers which were the accounting profession's bread and butter – were doing it themselves. In computerate countries, tax bureaux began to provide information, and even tax forms, in the form of computer software to plug directly into the home computer. Graham remembered an accounting colleague complaining that he now understood how scribes must have felt when everybody learned how to read and write.

Late in the 1990s, Graham was forced to supplement his falling income by taking a part-time teaching job, teaching adults the rudiments of accounting and finance. The vast majority of his students were the kinds of people who had comprised his former clients. They tended to be the very professionals and small business people who had acquired the computer capacity to do their own finance, but who needed a better grasp of the procedures. In addition, there would be a number of younger people in the process of starting up their own business.

Much to Graham's surprise, he really enjoyed the experience. He realized early on that his main function as a teacher was not to pour out a lot of knowledge, but to provide sympathetic support. He not only taught the students how to use the expert systems, but also, more importantly, to trust their own judgement. He understood that he could not compete with the expert systems (available to everybody) in terms of providing information, especially up-to-date information. Rather, what he offered was the human touch – in particular, a kind of fatherly reassurance that the students were really clever enough to handle the system.

It was not unnatural therefore, that he ended up in teaching as his second career. Now he was starting to move into his third. One of his interests had been history and archaeology. Not surprisingly, living in the North of England, he had become fascinated with industrial archaeology. Bradford, a rural village in the late eighteenth century had become a mighty industrial city in Victorian times – the 'wool capital' of the world. As Western society moved deeper into the Information Period, a great nostalgia developed for the earlier, apparently simpler, Industrial Period. People, not only in Western, but also in other countries, had begun to take a serious interest in the Industrial Revolution. Educational Tourism had become a major growth industry in many parts of the world. It was particularly successful in Bradford.

Graham's friend, Albert Teasdale, who had organized a thriving company catering for such tourists coming to the Yorkshire area had asked him to join the company as Education Manager. One reason for Albert's success had been that he had developed a happy mix of trips to interesting sites, with entertaining lectures explaining the history, geography, customs, and other aspects of the sites visited.

Albert was a shrewd businessman. He had known Graham since they were schoolboys together in the good old days. Talk to Albert about the good old days: Hah! You sat straight at your desk in straight rows, while the teacher shovelled a lot of rubbish at you for 45 or 50 minutes. They didn't seem to care what they taught you. As long as you didn't like it. They talked at you, or, as some were prone to, talked to the blackboard. Albert remembered falling asleep, dreaming of riding a horse across the moors.

At university, Albert had never approved of Graham going into accounting. 'Graham is a people's man . . .', he would announce to the assemblage of friends at the local pub 'not a figures man'. He would down his pint of Old Theakstons in one breath to prove the point. Albert's expanding business could use a man who was good both with figures and with people. Albert knew that Graham would not refuse the offer.

He was right. It wasn't the increase in salary, which was not very great in any case. It was the chance to do professionally what Graham had been doing as an amateur. He would be able to teach people from all over the world; he would train other teachers; he would go on field trips to find new sites to take the tourists to; he would go through old archives not yet found in computer data bases to uncover more historical material; he would liaise with museums and libraries all over the world. He would educate others. He would educate himself. He loved the idea.

The job would not start until the end of the present term. For the moment, Graham was content to talk to his computer, searching historical data bases for Bradford's role in the Industrial Revolution.

His musing was interrupted by the three older children setting off for the bus stop. Jill and John were friends again, as they discussed the difficulties she had faced with her house. Now that the problem was solved she felt much happier and could view John in a rosier light in spite of the fact he was humming *Eleanor Rigby*. Tim was quiet, hugging himself as he anticipated his class's reaction to his 'find'. Who could have thought he would have such luck. Good old Grandma. At the bus stop the three separated and went to join their friends already waiting for the bus.

Once in school, Jill made straight for the swimming pool. She found the synchronized team already hard at work. To her dismay she realized that Sheila Finn was swimming in the group. She feigned indifference and wandered over to Miss Martin's side. Miss Martin glanced down at her but continued to shout instructions into the computer on her wrist. This relayed messages into the hydrophones and earpieces of the swimmers. They obediently carried out her command. 'Miss Martin,' Jill said softly. Miss Martin did not respond. Again, 'Miss Martin', this time much louder. An edge had crept into her voice as she noticed that Sheila was fitting rather well into the pattern of the team. Miss Martin glanced down, 'Yes Jill, what is it?', she remarked, knowing quite well the reason for Jill's presence. 'Is Sheila Finn in the team?', she asked nervously, 'I had hoped you would consider me. Aren't I good enough?' Miss Martin continued watching the team, but said, 'Look Jill, these girls all come to school every morning. You, on your parent's insistence come to school in the afternoon. How can you expect to work with this team when you put in an appearance at this time of day? These girls have been working for two hours in the water. If you can persuade your parents to allow you to come to school for at least a few mornings I will give you a try out. You are a good swimmer, but there is no doubt about it, the afternoon swimmers are not as good as this group.' Jill's heart sank. She knew her parents liked all the family together at home during the morning. She answered, 'I'll talk to Mum about it,' her mind racing, trying to figure out what to do. 'Could you speak to her? If you told her you thought I would do well I'm sure she would listen to you.' Miss Martin looked at the anxious young face beside her. 'All right,' she said. 'Put your mother's computer number on your screen and I will contact her when I have finished here. In the meantime go and look at Program 45 and try out those manoeuvres as soon as you have changed into your swimming costume.' Miss Martin smiled at Jill who beamed back at her and ran off to get ready for her lesson. First she went to the screen of her micro and put not only her mother's number on it, but also her Dad's and grandparents' codes beside their location. There could be no possibility of her mother missing the message, even if her own screen was in use, the message would flash up into a corner of the screen and then her mother could respond when she had finished working.

After swimming, Jill had group work. On the way to the group she thought that she should have had Miss Martin talk to her father. Mum was a tough nut to crack. Maybe Grandad would help. As she entered the room, her friend Louise sauntered up: 'Ca va?', said

THE THREE Cs

Louise. 'Bah!', replied Jill. She was in no mood for French. Doubly so, with Sheila Finn in the group. Not only was Sheila good in French, she also knew French geography since she spent most summers there. Bah! She hated Sheila.

The group was currently studying French, France, and the people of France. They were engaged in a French simulation exercise. This would automatically be videoed for viewing by the French teacher. In addition, the history and geography teachers would also view the video since French history and geography were incorporated into their work. When the work was advanced enough, they would work on Euronet with children in Lyon who were studying English. Lyon was one of the French cities 'twinned' with Bradford.

While Jill was busy with French, and hating Sheila, John had a different problem. He had made his way into the Main Building. Most of his friends were already working. The trouble with living on the outskirts of Bradford was that his friends, who mostly lived in the centre of the city, could get to school at any time during the day or evening. Their production was well advanced. They were simulating life in Dallas during the time of President Kennedy's assassination. They had studied film, videos, and archive material on the last fatal hour of the President. Some of the group were plotting the shooting, others were the FBI, and a third group, President Kennedy's entourage. John had again used his musical skill to use Elvis Presley's music. He did not particularly like the music, but he had mixed it with 'Country and Western' so it did not sound quite so bad.

The group who were plotting the assassination were led by Helen. She was a beautiful girl of fifteen. Naturally she was a magnet for all the boys in the group, but she treated all of them alike. John watched her working. His heart was aching for her. He put his music on and asked his friend Al to watch it for a while. Al was great with electronics − but not the sort of person one could talk to about Helen. John missed his best friend Ken. Ken would be good to talk to, but Ken was off in Moscow for a six-months' study tour. Perhaps Dad would let John talk to Ken tonight on Euronet. But it would be hurried, and certainly not very private. So John wandered off to collect his thoughts. Halfway down the hall he changed his

180

mind: he found an empty study room. From the school's central data base, he called one of the Lifeskill programs onto the computer. He then described to the computer Helen's likes and dislikes. He talked about his own. In a short time, questions appeared on the screen. Rather selfconsciously he began to answer the questions, but it was very private and the answers were so encouraging. There in the privacy of the room he found some help from the computer on how to attract and hold Helen's attention. He was determined he would try the suggestions out at the first opportunity. He joined his friends who, by now, had decided to investigate the supposition that Kennedy's assassination was the work of some unidentified group of extremists. John tried to work it so that he would be made the FBI agent who had to question Helen as the leader of the extremists.

Tim was excited. He and his friends had watched the group of six students show their work on the Caribbean. That group was composed of three students of West Indian origin who were taking the other three to Jamaica for six months – the same way as Tim was one of six going to Pakistan for half a year. Their work was good and, had it not been for Tim's secret, he was certain the Caribbean group would have won the competition. They finished their work and Tim and his group jumped up. The group presentation was led by George, Tim's best friend. All went smoothly. It began during World War II. The Indian subcontinent was under British rule. Their presentation was to describe the formation of India and Pakistan and independence in 1947. Just as Tim had hoped, his *coup de grâce* was fantastic. At the appropriate moment he opened his bag and presented a whole series of old photographs and articles on Gandhi. His Grandmother's father had been in India during the struggle for independence. Magazines and photographs had been kept by his Grandmother as several of them showed her father, who had been on Lord Mountbatten's staff.

The other students were fascinated. They crowded round the albums of magazines. 'Obviously, Tim, your team has made the best presentation. Congratulations', said their teacher. 'When you go to Pakistan you will find the village you stay in is very different from those you are seeing in these pictures. Just think when your Grandma was a young girl she learned to read using books and magazines like these.' Tim grinned and said, 'I know, she keeps telling us.' His friends accepted the congratulations that were their due, discussed their next assignment from their teacher entitled 'Life in the Year 2040' and ran off to change for their game of football against the nearby High School.

Andrew and his grandfather walked slowly down the road. They kicked a stone gently to each other as they ambled along. Andrew, at four years old, was going to nursery and his grandfather went along to help. Andrew enjoyed having his grandfather with him, not that he spent much time with him. Other children who didn't have a grandparent needed Grandfather. He spent half his time in their home as a private tutor, the rest of his work time he spent in the nursery. The nursery, although Andrew did not notice it, was multiracial and his grandad taught English, Urdu, French, or Italian to groups of children. Nursery education extended to 7 years old and children were expected to be fluent in at least one other language before they moved on to Lower School. Parents chose the second language of their children. Andrew was learning Dutch. As he was one of a family of five children and four adults, they seemed to be a right United Nations. They all learned a different language so on travelling abroad they could find their way around. Andrew did some painting and modelling. His teacher changed his programs and he then went on to his Dutch class.

Mrs Hobart and Clare spent the afternoon in front of a computer. Since deciding on the Scottish holiday they had found out that the temperature was going to average about 14°C so they were buying some new clothes. It was also going to rain on the Tuesday so they bought a new umbrella and wellingtons for Mr Hobart. As a special treat they had bought some new luggage in a sale advertised on Prestel. The message from Jill's teacher had shown on the screen and Clare had been non-committal. She had informed Miss Martin she would discuss it with her husband when he arrived home that evening. Grandma then had a shock, she had been idly looking through the *Edinburgh Gazette*. On the computer she pressed the keys and the paper turned over. In the 'Deaths' column was the announcement of Peter Morris's death. She was so distressed as she remembered how close she had been to marrying him while they had studied at Aberdeen University. Tears streamed down her face and Clare was so sorry for her. She put her arm round her mother-in-law and asked the robot to bring a pot of tea and a small brandy. Later when Grandfather returned from the nursery they both went to their room and looked at the program entitled 'Who's Afraid of Death?' Peter's death had shocked them. It reminded them of their own mortality. After working through the program they felt better, having explored their own feelings openly, and together. They also felt secure in the knowledge that on current form they were both destined to live at least for ten more years, barring accidents, and if they chose to do so.

At dinner that evening the family met as usual. Wendy had had her supper and was settled for the evening. Graham announced the change in timetable for John and Jill. It was agreed they could both spend more time in the morning at school, and spend the afternoon at home. Tim was excitedly telling Grandmother all about his successful competition. The grandparents were both slightly tipsy. One small brandy had led to another. After dinner most of the family went to the school community centre. Graham and Clare were going to the driving range to improve their golf for the coming season. Jill was going to watch a video with some friends. The grandparents were going to meet their friends for a game of whist. Wendy, Andrew, and Tim would be all right. The sensors and the security robot would patrol the house. The bleeper on Graham's wrist would warn him of any problems. John went to the disco where he was hoping to meet Helen. He desperately wanted two things: Helen, and a Beatles revival.

After they all left, Tim settled down with his electronic book. It could be plugged into the holographic video box providing the full drama of his Wild West story. He fell asleep on the couch, dreaming of being grown-up – a man among men . . . . His sleep, though not his dreams, registered on Graham's and Clare's wrist monitors. When they returned home they cuddled him into bed.

Chapter 13

The Future: Dangers and Opportunities

The previous chapter represents a glimpse of the future. It describes what a successful, highly motivated, affluent, middle-class family might be doing with the new information technology. Clearly this is a family which has adapted well to the information age. Presumably, it is no less human for doing so. The question arises, however, are they part of an information elite? Are there other families or households, trapped into a vicious circle of poverty and ignorance, unable to avail themselves of the advantages of the new technology? Our view is that, whereas the late 1980s and early 1990s will see a polarization between the 'information-haves' and the 'information-have-nots', by the year 2010, those divisions will have eroded. Not only is the trend in Western societies for the middle classes to expand and comprise a larger and larger share of the population, but also, and more importantly, the new technology will become so cheap, and so potent that, like electricity, it will permeate virtually all homes.

People generally are not aware, how much of our daily home life is now dependent on electricity. We take for granted the light it provides. For many, it also provides a major source of heat, or of cooling (air conditioning). What most people don't realize is how many electric motors there are in the average home. The average reader of this book will probably have at least a dozen, perhaps twenty, electric motors in his or her home. Try counting them: in the refrigerator, washing machine, cleaner, other appliances, electric clocks, tape players, pumps in the water and heating systems, etc. Many of these motors, for example, those in clocks, are now being displaced by computers providing digital timepieces.

Electricity has also provided the basis for the home's communication systems. Fifty years ago, the average Western home would have a radio, perhaps a record player, and, in the USA, a telephone. Since then, tape players, television sets, and now, video recorders have become commonplace. Instead of one radio per household, it's now closer to one radio per room (including, often, one in the family car). Most dramatic was the introduction of television in the 1950s. Within about a decade the situation shifted from practically nobody owning a set to the majority of households possessing one.

It will be the same with computers. Not only are they finding their way into the home's clocks, heating systems, radios, light switches, all appliances, etc., but by the turn of the century the vast majority of homes will also own several personal computers.

If we wish to look twenty-five years ahead, and if we assume that there will be as much progress as over the past twenty-five years, then with 1985 as our base line, we should start with 1960. In 1960 neither pocket calculators nor digital watches were known. The chip as we have come to know it, also did not exist. Micro-electronics had moved the computer technology off electronic valves onto transistors and then onto integrated circuits. Television had become a reality in most households – but just. The idea of having men walk on the moon still seemed science fiction to most people.

We are making a mistake, however, if we assume that the rate of progress is linear. It is exponential. It is probably more accurate to say that if you want to look twenty-five years into the future, you must look fifty years into the past. That would bring us to 1935. In 1935 there were no more than a handful of men around the world who had any idea of the possibility of computers becoming a reality. And, in any case, computers in those days were viewed as very large machines of the type that did, in fact, make their appearance in the 1940s. The early computers required an entire hall for their housing. In 1935, television was known only to very few, and was certainly never envisioned as a common household device. Only a minority of households had a telephone. Advanced electronics and communication devices were thought of more as science fiction than as reality. Twenty years later, in 1955, computers were just emerging from the dinosaur age, i.e. they were still largely big frames with small brains. Even people as clever and talented as Isaac Asimov, who thought about the future in advanced science fiction terms, had no inkling of the chip – nor that, by the 1980s, people would be walking around with computers in their pockets and on their wrists.

With this as background, it must be clear how difficult it is to project twenty-five years into the future. All sorts of inventions and principles may be discovered in the next twenty-five years of which we have no inkling at the moment. Nevertheless, there are broad trends perceivable in information technology. It may be that the projections turn out to be inaccurate. It is highly probable that some of the things we envision will happen much earlier. A few may happen later. Some may not happen at all. And, undoubtedly, some will happen that we have not even discussed. Nevertheless, it is a useful device to focus on what is likely to be happening over the next generation: for it is that generation which we must educate for a new world.

Over the next fifteen years we can realistically look to rapid advances in technology in at least four interrelated areas. First, the microcomputers themselves will become very powerful and very cheap. They will have very large memories, and you will be able to talk to them. Second, there will emerge a host of cheap peripherals, from computer toys to communication devices, including cheap printers, Viewdata, cable TV, and satellite systems. Third, in parallel, there will emerge a host of electronic data bases around the world such as the *Oxford English Dictionary*, the *Encyclopaedia Britannica*, the *New York Times*, and the *Financial Times*, as well as libraries, museums, specialist archives, government bureaux, etc. Last, but not least, there will emerge a flood of professional education software, authored by some of the best brains in the world, including those working on artificial intelligence.

Left to its own devices, this process of technological evolution could have a negative impact on society. Clearly, the computer and ancillary technology will invade the home and alter the education system in a way unparalleled in previous education history. This leads to a number of questions, both practical and social. Among the practical questions, we need to know what are the most appropriate reward systems for motivating children to learn with the help of computers. How does the use of humour affect learning? The studies of Davies and Apter [1] clearly show that 'humour can be used in such a way as to aid learning.' However, these authors, as well as others provide ample evidence that humour used inappropriately either adds nothing to the learning experience, or may actually detract from it.

The problem extends beyond humour. Do all audio or visual rewards reinforce the learning experience, or do they distract? Are such rewards merely frivolous? Might computer-based learning systems hinder certain kinds of learning? Might they inhibit genuine curiosity? Might they undermine long-term interests in a topic?

At the social level we should ask: what will be the impact on society? What will be the impact on children? Will the violence observed on computer screens reinforce violent behaviour? Will the anthropomorphization of computers and, in due course, of robot toys, cause children to behave like robots themselves? Alternatively, if the computer or robot is the perfect slave to be turned on and off at will, will children confuse accepted behaviour with real people? What about the incredible amounts of information which will comprise the environment of children of the future, will it cause information overload? What are the symptoms and pathologies of information overload? The hypnotic effect of computers is well-known. In the United States there is a phenomenon called computer divorce, where one spouse, so intrigued with working with a computer, begins to overlook the responsibilities and affections due other members of the household. Lastly, a very real problem is shaping up in the technologically advanced countries where middle-class families will avail themselves of this new technology to give their children maximum educational advantages. Will this lead to a new polarization in Western societies between the 'information-haves' and the 'information-have-nots'.

THE THREE Cs

COMPUTERS FOR EVERYBODY

The education of its citizens is the duty of the State. (The Constitution of Greece)

The answer to avoiding polarization of society into the information-rich and information-poor is for the state to ensure that all children have their own personal computer. In affluent countries, governments ought to provide *two* computer systems for each child: one at home, and one in school.

Such a scheme may sound incredibly expensive. However, let us do a few calculations, using the UK as an example. About 40 per cent of the UK's population of 56 million is under 16, i.e. about 23 million youngsters. If the government were to engage in a policy of two personal computers for every child (one for the home, one at school), the UK would need a maximum of 46 million units. However, one would probably only need about 30 million if one limited the computers to one unit per household (i.e. children sharing them at home) and provided computers only to children over the age of four. Actually, considering the size and weight of the computer keyboards, only one portable computer, to be carried back and forth, could be a practical alternative. We are therefore talking about 20 to 30 million units. If the government decided on a single mass-produced model, a cost of £100 per system would buy not only the computer but also printers and modems, plus a black and white display unit, where needed. Most homes have television; most homes with children have telephones. Special grants might be needed for the small percentage of deprived homes lacking TV or telephones. The total direct cost to the government would therefore be of the order of £3,000 million.

One could not carry out such a programme within a year or two. It should be phased in over a period of six years. Spread over six years, the budget would require on average £500 million per year. During the mid-1980s that would represent of the order of 5 per cent of the revenue the UK government collects on North Sea oil.

Such a program would boost the economy, in general, and the information technology industry, in particular. It would generate jobs and stimulate the kind of economic activity which would repay the government in terms of decreased unemployment, decreased crime and other social costs, and increased revenues. It would represent one of the soundest investments any country can make in its economic future.

THE ECONOMICS OF EDUCATION

Towards the end of the eighteenth century, agriculture was still dominant. The ownership of land was of prime importance and the vast bulk of the labour force was still working on farms. It is no wonder that many were dazzled by the pre-eminence of the agricultural sector of the economy. In retrospect, we can see that the economy of Adam Smith's day was beginning to slip into a 'post-agricultural' economy. In Queen Victoria's heyday, under the pressure of advancing technology, Great Britain had shifted to an industrial economy. From being an exporter of food, she had become a net importer. Political power had shifted from the landed aristocrat to the capitalist. The bulk of the labour force was no longer employed on the land. Manufacture and trade, not agriculture, accounted for the biggest share of the country's productive potential.

Today we have witnessed a similar shift. Political power is shifting from the owners of capital to the professional bureaucrats and technocrats – the purveyors of information. Only a shrinking minority of the labour force toils in factories; and the service sector has overtaken manufacture in terms of the country's gross national product. We now live in a post-industrial economy [2].

There exists no productive labour input which does not, at the same time, involve an input of information. Futhermore, information, like capital, can be accumulated and stored for future use. In a post-industrial society, a country's store of information is its principal asset, its greatest potential source of wealth. In a post-industrial economy the basic principle of new wealth creation depends on the conversion of 'non-resources' into useful products. Oil under the North Sea, and desert land reclamation are but two such examples.

People create wealth. Human capital is the most important

resource of post-industrial societies. It is through technological expertise and organizational competence that new, wealth-creating systems come into existence. Technological expertise and managerial competence need to be backed up by a skilled labour force to implement the development of new systems. In addition to these skills, the development of new productive systems also requires a very different kind of skill. This is a form of business acumen which understands market opportunities and how to exploit them. It is the assured sale of a product or service which motivates its development. This is true even if it is a charitable or government-run enterprise.

At the base of all skills, competence, and expertise is education. In its broadest sense, education includes the sum total accumulation of information by an individual, including practical experience. The best strategy to effect a smooth transition from an industrial to an information economy is by means of a massive expansion of both education, and research and development. The latter should be aimed at creating the wealth necessary to support expansion of the public service sector (government-run) economy. The expansion of the former, education, is required: to upgrade the human capital to make the workforce economically more productive, ranging from manual labour to theoretical scientists; to create an informed citizenry capable of manoeuvring effectively in an information economy; and to keep everybody from going neurotic in a rapidly changing information environment.

Any object or material can be made more valuable by adding information: waste desert land plus information becomes productive crop land. Idle capital plus information becomes revenue-yielding investment. Useless energy like sunshine or ocean waves can be made to perform useful work when you know how. Ignorant labourers plus education become skilled, highly productive operatives. The reason why education, as an industry, continues to command an ever-increasing share of the nation's wealth (ignoring minor and temporary government cuts) is that education adds information to people, thereby increasing their economic value. Over the next few decades education will grow to become the largest industry in post-industrial societies – and its number one employer.

190

American farmers are perhaps the most productive in the world today. They work from an enormous information base which has accumulated over centuries. To utilize it properly they must know about fertilizer and soil conditions, hybrid seeds and crop rotation, insecticides and weed killers, and how to select a tractor, drive a combine-harvester, maintain farming machinery, haggle with commodity speculators who will pay for a crop before it is planted, keep records and accounts, organize cooperatives to build storage silos, follow the latest technological developments, etc., etc. If they deal with livestock, they will know about hybrid cattle and antibiotics, and may run a computer to optimize feeding routines. If they grow crops, no longer do they plant one crop year after year as their fathers and grandfathers did before them. It's wheat one year, maize the next and soya beans the year after that, depending on the price they can get from a food processing firm, or from a grain speculator whose information reveals what commodities are likely to be in short supply next year.

American farmers of today usually have a university degree and know how to be a part-time cultivator, mechanic, veterinarian or plant pathologist, soil chemist, computer operator, accountant, and manager. By the late 1970s the average world farmer fed five people, while the average Western European farmer fed twenty. The average American farmer fed close to sixty.

Education is also of great value to Third World farmers. Farmers with four years of primary education produce about 13 per cent more than those without education. Between 1950 and 1975, adult literacy in middle-income developing countries rose from 48 to 71 per cent. In low-income countries it rose from 22 to 38 per cent. The fastest-developing countries had above average literacy rates. Literacy contributes to increased output per worker and increased investment.

Educating girls may be one of the best investments a country can make in future growth. Even if girls never enter the labour force, it is mothers rather than fathers whose influences are crucial for children. In addition, educated women marry later and are more likely to know about family planning. In Brazil, families were better fed the higher the mother's education.

THE THREE Cs

We pointed out above the danger of creating a polarization in Western societies between the 'information-haves' and the 'information-have-nots'. The same may be said for global society. Affluent societies with a good education infrastructure will avail themselves of the new education technology. Third World countries may lack either the education infrastructure, or the necessary financial resources, or both. Thus the advances in education fostered by the new information technology may widen the gap and greatly exacerbate the divisions already existing in global society.

There is, however, another possibility. Computer-based systems may allow Third World countries to leapfrog over Western systems. At the moment, most Third World countries are mimicking Western systems, often twenty years behind the times. Considering that much of Western education is itself largely out of date, the impact on Third World countries may be crippling to their intellectual development. Keeping in mind the importance of human capital as a country's major resource, that could be disastrous.

Solar-powered pocket calculators can be bought relatively cheaply. Solar-powered computers, therefore, could become a cost-effective alternative to building schools in remote locations and staffing them with third-rate teachers. Both the Open University in the UK, and China's TV University represent successful experiments in distance learning. India has been experimenting with education via satellites. Putting solar-powered computers into hamlets and villages, and supplying them with software via television or satellite, or conventionally with tapes, disks, or cartridges, could prove to be highly advantageous. Depending on the culture, one should train within each village or hamlet, the high-status individuals, preferably grandmothers and grandfathers. Where there already exist schools with teachers, retrain the teachers. The TV units could be used both as computer VDUs or for direct TV broadcasts. The electronic grandmother system would provide the widest possible range of subjects – teaching young children (and adults) literacy, mothers about nutrition, farmers about animal husbandry, university students about calculus, etc. District inspectors would roam the countryside providing support and help, including replacing faulty equipment which would be repaired at district headquarters. Such inspectors could also monitor the progress of the children and advise the government education service about problems or further improvements. There would need to be a major national facility which adapts computers and video programs imported from other countries, and which develops its own material. The national centre, and perhaps all the regional centres, would be plugged into the various global data bases described earlier.

Such a system would not only allow Third World education systems to catch up with the West, but all countries would also be able to keep abreast of the latest developments. In some instances, a country would be able to innovate and pioneer, thereby moving ahead of its Western counterparts.

These electronic education systems would also greatly facilitate technology transfer. Courses developed by the Open University in England, or the TV University in China, would, with minor modifications, be applicable to most, perhaps all, countries. To import electronically based information would be cheaper than to import (or produce!) text books. Specialist courses developed on computer by one university, could be instantly shared around the world. Best of all, we would be creating a global education system, vital to creating a global culture − and to peace.

The Western countries could be of greatest service to their Third World cousins if they helped fund and institute such electronic education systems. Whether or not there will develop an enlightened public opinion in the West which will force political leaders to carry out such a mission remains to be seen.

HOMO SAPIENS CEREBRUS

Irrespective of whether enlightened government policies prevail over the next few years, sooner or later all children, first in the technologically advanced societies, then all over the world, will have personal computers at home and access to computer systems at school. Children who have an early experience with computers will develop a technical expertise as second nature. One of the sources of amazement to teachers and parents watching young children working with computers is the rapidity with which they learn how to program, run a tape recorder, and carry out all the procedures necessary for making a computer work. In part, this astonishment reflects our own cultural experience; we overlook the fact that early in the nineteenth century, five-year-old children used to work machinery in the industrial mills of Northern England, and that in Third World countries, five-year-olds will have significant responsibilities — the girls in bringing up younger siblings, the boys in taking care of the family cattle, or in other ways helping out. A helpless childhood is a Western construct.

Perhaps the most important impact computers will have is teaching children how to think more effectively. Seymour Papert [3] complains that our tendency is to categorize children into smart and dumb people when, in fact, it is often a question of context and experience. Working out flow charts, developing habits of precision and discipline, building in checks, carrying out sub-routines in order to build larger structures, all of these foster intellectual qualities which are not produced in the same way in the present system. We know that handicapped children have shown substantial improvements in IQ tests when given the proper tools. This principle will be found applicable to virtually all children. The human mind is an exquisite information processing device reflecting the evolution of intelligence over a period of a billion years.

The late Chris Evans believed that the scale of intelligence should begin with a rock or some other inert matter which has zero intelligence, then work up from an amoeba which clearly has enough intelligence to move away from an undesirable environment and towards a more desirable one, up through a variety of invertebrates to fish, amphibians, etc., up to the mammals. Finally, we should look at our closest relative, the chimp, which one can teach the rudiments of logic with little difficulty. Human intelligence, excluding brain-damaged individuals, is well above that.

Undoubtedly, intelligence by whatever definition, when measured by any single test, or even a combination of tests, will show a statistical variation around some mean. However, that

194

variation has been blown up out of all proportion. If today we can teach chimps the rudiments of logic, what will we be able to teach them when we understand both chimps and teaching better? And when we understand teaching better, what will we be able to teach humans? Consider that young children practically teach themselves a language. What an incredible intellectual feat! Thousands of words, phonology, phraseology, sentence structure, syntax, semantics – it all comes naturally! Furthermore, with modern understanding of the human *body*, improvements in medicine, nutrition, exercises, etc. have produced populations who are taller than their parents, are healthier, live longer, and whose athletes out-perform the best of the older generations. The same will happen as we learn to understand how the brain works. The human brain can accomplish much more than answer questions on intelligence tests contrived by experts who have about as much understanding of how the brain works as the ancient Greeks had of the functioning of the human body.

The high motivational state induced in children working with good education software, coupled to the emergence of a global network of data bases which allow the child access to information with unprecedented ease, must have an impact on the understanding children develop of the world they live in and, for that matter, in understanding themselves. Furthermore, as indicated above, children encouraged to write their own programs will develop intellectual skills of precision and logic, a systematic and orderly method for producing work, and a much more sophisticated approach to the methods for solving problems. Not only that, but, contrary to popular feelings, computers will *enhance* the creative impulses of children. The cumulative improvements in intellectual skills and creativity, coupled to a markedly expanded understanding of the world, will differentiate such children almost to the extent of their forming a new sub-species: *Homo sapiens cerebrus*, or some such.

The matter is analogous to a situation prevailing perhaps between five and ten million years ago, when our pre-human hominid ancestors began to use weapons, both to ward off predators and subdue prey. That earliest of all technological revolutions differentiated the hominid stock from the rest of the primates. The hominids were able to extend their econiche to hunting large game. In due course, as they mastered fire, they were able to extend their geographic range more successfully than any other primate.

In human history it was always those who were able to develop and use new technologies adroitly who in the long run not only survived better, but also came to dominate the others. *Homo sapiens cerebrus* will survive, prosper, and in due course dominate all those who do not partake of the new intellectual technology. Among higher organisms, new behaviour patterns, rather then new anatomical features, set the stage for new patterns of evolution. The computer is setting the stage for a revolution as profound as the hominid revolution of a half a dozen, or so, million years ago. Will we be able to cope with it?

References to Books or Periodicals

CHAPTER 1

[1] *Home Views* H84–7, p. 3. Future Computing Inc., US 1984.
[2] *Talmis Industry Update.* July 1984.
[3] *Cowling Marketing Services.* London, 1984.

CHAPTER 2

[1] *Mindstorms: Children, Computers and Powerful Ideas*, Seymour Papert. Harvester Press, 1981.
[2] See also *Turtle Geometry*, Harold Abelson and Andrea di Sessa. The MIT Press, 1981.

CHAPTER 3

[1] *The Second Self*, Sherry Turkle. Simon & Schuster, 1984.

CHAPTER 4

[1] G.M. Mills, 'Categories of educational microcomputer programs, theories of learning and implications for future research'. In B.S. Alloway and G.M. Mills (eds), *Aspects of Educational Techology XVIII*. Kogan Page, 1985.

CHAPTER 5

[1] *Talking and Learning*, Joan Tough. Ward Lock Educational, 1977.
[2] *How Children Learn*, John Holt. Penguin Books, 1970.
[3] Michael Armstrong, *Closely Observed Children*. Camelian Press, 1980.
[4] *Reading*, Frank Smith. Cambridge University Press, 1978, p. 6.
[5] Frank Smith, *Reading*, p. 4.
[6] Frank Smith, *Reading*, p. 7.
[7] Frank Smith, *Reading*, p. 19.

THE THREE Cs

CHAPTER 6

[1]   Frank Smith, *Reading*. Cambridge University Press, 1978, p. 12.
[2]   Don Clark, 'A world in a grain of sand'. In *Exploring English with Microcomputers*, Daniel Chandler (ed.). Council for Education Technology, 1983, pp. 37–41.
[3]   Seymour Papert, *Mindstorms*. Harvester Press, 1981, p. 31.
[4]   *Language and the Primary School*. National Association of Headteachers, Haywards Heath, W. Sussex, p. 29.
[5]   Frank Smith, *Reading*, pp. 138–142.
[6]   Frank Smith, *Reading*, p. 74.
[7]   Peggy O'Brien, 'Using microcomputers in the writing class'. *The Computing Teacher*, May 1984, pp. 20–21.
[8]   Seymour Papert, *Mindstorms*, p. 30.
[9]   See reviews in *Educational Computing*, February 1984.

CHAPTER 7

[1]   M. Sharples and D. McConnell, 'Distance teaching by CYCLOPS: An educational evaluation of the Open University's tele-writing system'. *Brit. Jour. Educ. Technol.*, March 1983.
[2]   Joseph Weizenbaum, 'ELIZA – A computer program for the study of natural language communication between man and machine'. *Communications of the ACM*, **9** (1), 36–45 (1965).
[3]   Bruce Lang Associates. Videodisc Application Consultants. Ave Perou 77, 1050 Brussels, Belgium.
[4]   Bert Camstra, 'Case study'. *Proc. 1st Int'l Confer. on New Technologies in Training* October 1984. Brintex Ltd, London, pp. 191–202.
[5]   *Times Higher Education Supplement*, 24 August 1984, p. 6.
[6]   Dr Roger Lucas, Psychologist/Director, Insight Evaluation Centre Limited, 11 Royal Crescent, GLASGOW G3 7SL.
[7]   Mildred L.G. Shaw, 'Interactive computer programs for eliciting personal models of the world'. Paper presented to the 2nd Int'l Congress on Personal Construct Theory, Christ Church College, Oxford, July 1977.
[8]   Mary Humphrey, 'All the scientists in the world smushed into one: What kids think about computers'. *Creative Computing*, April, 1982, pp. 96–98.
[9]   Colin Price, School of Science and Society, University of Bradford, Bradford BD7 1DP (postgraduate work in progress, 1984).

CHAPTER 8

[1]   Electronic Learning Machine (ELM) System, Format Peripherals Ltd, 25 Bridge Street, Rothwell, KETTERING, Northants.

CHAPTER 9

[1]   Warnock, 'Special educational needs: Report of the Committee of Enquiry'. HMSO, Cmnd No. 7212, May 1978.

[2] As reported at the World Conference on Computers and Education, Lausanne, July 1981.

[3] *Proceedings Ninth Australian Computer Conference*, Hobart, 1982, p. 151.

[4] *Special Technology for Special Children*, E. Paul Goldenberg. University Park Press, Baltimore, 1979, p. 126.

[5] *Microcomputers and Special Education: A Guide to Good Practice*, Bob Hogg. National Council for Special Education, Stratford-on-Avon, 1984.

[6] *Microcomputers in Special Education*, F. Green, R. Hart, C. McCall, and I. Staples. Longmans/Schools Council, 1982.

[7] Warnock, op. cit.

CHAPTER 10

[1] J. Tizard, W.N. Schofield, and J. Hewison, 'Collaboration between teachers and parents in assessing children's reading'. *Educational Psychology*, **52**, 1–15 (1982).

[2] Alan Brown and Fiona Brown, 'The computer in the home'. *Proceedings, Ninth Australian Computer Conference*, Hobart, 1982, pp. 217–222.

CHAPTER 11

[1] Christopher Evans, *The Mighty Micro*. Victor Gollancz, 1979, Chapter 8.

[2] Alan Kay and Adele Goldberg, 'Personal dynamic media'. *Computer* March 1977, pp. 31–41. (Also *XEROX PARC Technical Report SSL-76.1*, March 1976.)

[3] Michael Sharples, *The Dynabook*. Unpublished manuscript, 1984.

[4] Michael Sharples, *Patterns of Words*. Unpublished manuscript, 1984.

[5] W.R. Bennett, Jr, 'How artificial is intelligence?' *American Scientist*, **65**, 694–702 (1977).

[6] E.J. Yannakoudakis and D. Fawthrop, 'The rules of spelling errors'. *Information Processing and Management*, **19** (2), pp. 87–99 (1983).

[7] E.J. Yannakoudakis and D. Fawthrop, 'An intelligent spelling error corrector'. *Information Processing and Management*, **19** (2), pp. 101–108 (1983).

[8] Interview with David Ahl. *Creative Computing*, **10** (8), 113 (1984).

[9] E.A. Feigenbaum and P. McCorduck, *The Fifth Generation*. Michael Joseph, 1984, p. 184.

[10] *Financial Times*, 3 July 1984.

]11] E.H. Shortcliffe, 'Medical consultation systems: Designing for doctors'. In *Designing for Human Computer Communication*, M.E. Sime and M.J. Coombs (eds). Academic Press, 1983, pp. 209–238.

[12] As reviewed by W.I. Card and R.W. Lucas, 'Computer interrogation in medical practice'. *Internat. J Man–Machine Studies*, **14**, 49–57 (1981).

[13] Christopher Evans, *The Mighty Micro*. Victor Gollancz, 1979, p. 113.

[14] M.J. Fritter and P.J. Cruikshank, 'Doctors using computers: A case study'. In *Designing for Human Computer Communication*, M.E. Sime and M.J. Coombs (eds). Academic Press, 1983, pp. 239–260.

[15] E.H. Shortcliffe, *op cit*.

[16] *Financial Times*, 29 August 1984.

THE THREE Cs

CHAPTER 12

[1] *Financial Times* 31 August 1984. Cybersoft Intelligent Systems, Canterbury 0227-60456.

CHAPTER 13

[1] A.P. Davies and M.J. Apter, 'Humour and its effect on learning in children'. In *Children's Humour*, P.E. McGhee and A.J. Chapman (eds). John Wiley (1980) pp. 237–253.
[2] Tom Stonier, *The Wealth of Information*, Thames/Methuen, 1983.
[3] Seymour Papert, *Mindstorms*. Harvester Press, 1981, p. 43.

Other, Related Writings of the Authors

Cathy Conlin

'Computers in Schools', Heinemann *Infants & Computers*, **4** (1), 15–16 (October 1981).
'Norton Glebe infants work with computers', Disbury School of Education Faculty of Community Studies, Manchester Polytechnic, *Greater Manchester Primary Contact*, **1** (2) p. 18–22 (1982).
'The impact of home and school microcomputers on primary, especially infant children', *Greater Manchester Primary Contact Special Issue*, No. 2, pp. 43–45 (1983).
'Micros made easy – how to start and what to expect', *Educational Computing*, 18–19 (December 1983).
'Micros made easy – five years on ... what next', *Educational Computing*, 22–23 (April 1984).
'Making faces', *Primary Teachers & Micros*, Scholastic Publications, 12–13 (May 1984).
'Desert Island Disk', *Primary Teachers & Micros*, Scholastic Publications, 22–23 (September 1984).
'Classroom management: A dozen bright ideas', pp. 22–23, 'Program reviews', pp. 36–39, *Primary Teachers & Micros* Scholastic Publications, (March 1985).

T. Stonier (1985)

'Computer psychology', *Education and Child Psychology*, **1** (2–3), 16–27 (1984).
'The computer: Most powerful educational technology ever?', *Proc. 18th Ann. Confer., Assoc. for Educational and Training Technology* (ETIC '84) (in press).
'Teaching and learning about science and society' (Opening keynote address), *Proc. 3rd Int. Symp. on World Trends in Science and Technology Education* (10–20 December '84, Brisbane, Australia) (in press).

T. Stonier (1984)

'Education returns to the home', *Data Processing*, **26** (2), 58–59 (1984).
'Thinking about thinking machines', *Creative Computing*, **10** (11), 252–254 (1984).
'The knowledge industry', in *Expert Systems*, R. Forsyth (ed), Chapman & Hall, London, 1984, pp. 221–226.

THE THREE Cs

T. Stonier (1983)

The Wealth of Information: A Profile of the Post-Industrial Economy, Thames/Methuen, 1983.
'The emerging education revolution', *Proc. Ninth International Conference on Improving University Teaching*, Dublin, University of Maryland, 1983, pp. 30–45.
'Teaching physics is not enough', *Physics Education*, **18** (3), 101–102 (1983).
'Changes in Western society: Educational implications', in *The International Schools Journal*, No. 6, pp. 7–21, European Council of International Schools, Autumn 1983. (Reprint of article, see T. Stonier (1979)).
Words, Words, Words (Education Software), Applied Systems Knowledge, London, 1983.

T. Stonier and D. Catlin (1983)

'The Valiant Turtle', in *Electronic Education*, **3** (3), 50, 52.

J. Shaylor and T. Stonier (1983)

'Evaluating educational software', *Educational Computing*, **4** (4) p. 9, May 1983.

T. Stonier (1982)

'The revolution in education', *Proc. 9th Australian Computer Society Conference*, Schools Symposium (Hobart, Tasmania), August 1982.
'Making the most of a switched-on society', *The Times Higher Education Supplement*, 21 May 1982.
'Changes in Western society: Educational implications', in *New Direction in Primary Education*, Colin Richards (ed.), The Falmer Press, 1982, pp. 287–300 (Reprint of article, see T. Stonier (1979)).

G.M. Mills and T. Stonier (1982)

'Trends and prospects for microcomputer-based eduation', in *International Journal of Man–Machine Studies*, **17**, 143–148 (1982).

T. Stonier (1981)

'The natural history of humanity: Past, present and future', in *International Journal of Man–Machine Studies*, **14**, 91–122 (1981). (Based on inaugural lecture, University of Bradford, 17 February 1976.)
'A little learning is a lucrative thing', *The Times Higher Education Supplement*, 1st May 1981.
'The rise and rise of the knowledge industry', in *Does I.T. Matter*, Robert Irvine Smith (ed.), Longman, 1981, pp. 7–8.
'Why we must swim with the tide of revolution', *The Teacher*, 23 October 1981, p. 3.

G. Poulter and T. Stonier (1981)

'Commercial programs can be useful aids', *Educational Computing*, **2** (10), 27 (1981).

T. Stonier (1980)

'Education and the 21st Century', *Times Educational Supplement*, 15 February 1980.

T. Stonier (1979)

'Changes in Western society: Educational implications', in *World Yearbook of Education 1979: Recurrent Education and Lifelong Learning*, T. Schuller and J. Megarry (eds), Kogan Page, London, pp. 31–44.

T. Stonier (1978)

'Educating for the future', *The Listener*, 28 September 1978, pp. 415–416.
'Education for the future', Discussion paper commissioned by the National Union of Teachers for a conference on 'Young people in transition: The education and training of 14–19 year olds', London, June, 1978.
'Oiling the wheels of a slick future', *The Education Guardian*, 3 May 1978.

Bibliography

Suggested further reading of books that have been helpful to the authors and provided background information. We have listed 30 out of thousands of books – it is obviously an arbitrary choice, much of it accidental. However, these books are useful for expanding most of the concepts discussed in *The Three Cs*. Almost all of the books listed are comprehensible to lay readers, although they may be addressed to specialist audiences. The first dozen or so, books would be particularly useful for structuring an introductory course for educators to teach the impact of computers on society, in general, and education, in particular.

1. *Mindstorms: Children, Computers and Powerful Ideas.* Seymour Papert. Harvester Press, 1981.
2. *The Mighty Micro.* Christopher Evans. Victor Gollancz, 1979.
3. *The Second Self: Computers and the Human Spirit.* Sherry Turkle. Simon and Schuster, New York, 1984.
4. *The Wealth of Information.* Tom Stonier. Thames/Methuen, 1983.
5. *The Making of the Micro.* Christopher Evans. Victor Gollancz, 1981.
6. *Young Learners and the Microcomputer.* Daniel Chandler. Open University Press, 1984.
7. *Exploring English with Microcomputers.* Daniel Chandler (ed). National Association for the Teaching of English (UK), Council for Education Technology, London, 1983.
8. *Microcomputers and Special Educational Needs: A Guide to Good Practice.* Bob Hogg. National Council for Special Education, Stratford-upon-Avon, 1984.
9. *Special Technology for Special Children.* Paul Goldenberg. University Park Press, Baltimore, 1979.
10. *An Introduction to Educational Computing.* N.J. Rushby. Croom-Helm, 1979.
11. *Computer World.* Jacquetta Megarry. Piper Books Ltd, 1983.
12. *Computers and Education.* World Yearbook of Education 1982/83. J. Megarry, D.R.F. Walker, S. Nisbet, and E. Hoyle (eds). Kogan Page, 1983.
13. *Microcomputers in Special Education.* F. Green, R. Hart, C. McCall and I. Staples. Longmans/Schools Council, 1982.
14. *Computers in Teaching Maths.* Peter Kelman. Addison Wesley, 1983.
15. *Microchild Learning through Logo.* Seraphim Gascoigne. Macmillan, 1984.
16. *Starting Logo.* Richard Noss. AUCBE, Hatfield, Herts., 1983.
17. *Big Trak Plus*, M.D. Meredith and B.I. Briggs, Council for Education Technology. 1982.

18. *The Penguin Computing Book*. Susan Curran and Ray Curnow. Penguin Books, 1983.
19. *The Micro Revolution Revisited*. Peter Large. Frances Pinter, London, 1984.
20. *How Children Learn*. John Holt. Penguin Books, 1970.
21. *How Children Fail*. John Holt. Penguin Books, 1969.
22. *Reading*. Frank Smith. Cambridge University Press, 1978.
23. *Learning to Read*. Margaret Meek. Bodley Head, 1977.
24. *Listening to Children Talking*. Joan Tough, Ward Lock Educational, 1976.
25. *Talking and Learning*. Joan Tough, Ward Lock Educational, 1977.
26. *Young Children Thinking*. Alice Yardley. Evans Brothers, 1973.
27. *Thought and Language*. L.S. Vygotsky. John Wiley, New York, 1962.
28. *The Needs of Children*. Kellmer Pringle. Hutchinson, 1974.
29. *Piaget Education and Training*. D.W. McNally. Harvester Press, 1977.
30. *Expert Systems*. Richard Forsyth (ed). Chapman & Hall, 1984.

Glossary

Artificial Intelligence: A system of problem-solving which is designed for robots and computers, resembling human behaviour in terms of learning, reasoning, etc.

Audio Visual Aids: Educational tools which help students to learn, e.g., audio cassettes, television, videos, computers, charts, slides, etc., which utilize the student's eyes or ears to reinforce teaching.

BASIC: A popular programming language used on most microcomputers in schools and at home. The language may vary slightly from one computer to another.

Bit: The smallest unit of information which may be represented by a '0' or '1', or a switch, in an ON or OFF position.

Bugs: A mistake in the program usually caused by errors in the actual format of the programming, e.g., in the language or a typing error. A bug may cause a program to crash.

Byte: A group of 8 bits representing one character of text, such as a letter, punctuation mark, or number.

Cathode Ray Tube (CRT): The American term for a television or computer screen. Same as VDU.

Character: Any symbol, e.g., a space, a letter, or a number used in a computer program.

Chip: A single integrated circuit contained on one small square sliver of silicon. The chip circuitry is equivalent to that which used to be contained on thousands of transistors.

Computer-aided Design (CAD): The computer is used to help designers, draughtsmen, artists, etc. in the process of designing plans, blueprints, textile patterns, etc.

Computer-assisted Instruction (CAI): The computer is used mainly as a drill and practice machine.

Computer-assisted Learning (CAL): The computer is used in an interactive teaching format.

Computer-based Education (CBE): What this book is about.

Computer-based Training (CBT): The computer is used to help teach specific skills. For example, pilots, train drivers, mechanics etc. may be confronted with computer-based simulations of real situations. Similar to *Computer-based Learning (CBL)*.

206

Computer-managed Learning (CML): Computers are used in this context as monitors, assessors, and reporters of the student or user's progress.

Computer Network: A linking of computers in schools, offices, or industry to transfer information from one to the other, or for groups of people to have access to identical information simultaneously.

Concept Keyboard: A specially devised keyboard usually containing only a few keys to facilitate the use of computers by young and, especially, handicapped children. Concept keyboards may actually contain more keys than the standard Qwerty keyboard when it is designed to achieve special functions or concepts.

Crash: The term used when, for no apparent reason, the computer program ceases to function.

Cursor: The flashing square or line on the computer, which points up the position on the screen where the next typed letter or mark will appear.

Data: Plural of datum. A datum is a single piece of information.

Data base: An organized source of information especially created on the computer. Information can be inserted or extracted.

Device: The computer or a peripheral such as a light pen, joystick, robot turtle, etc., which processes or communicates information.

Disk(c)(ette) (floppy): Similar to a music record but capable of storing large amounts of information which can be rapidly stored or retrieved by the computer.

Distance Learning: As in the UK's Open University or China's Radio and Television University. A system of learning where the teaching is via computer, television, or video − at a distance.

Documentation: Necessary information included with a computer program describing aims, objectives, and running of the program. This also refers to manuals of instruction for every computer.

Drill and Practice: Such programs are devised to reinforce learning, e.g. spellings, tables, number bonds, etc., by simple question and answer techniques.

Educational Computing: Learning from the computer rather than programming it.

Expert Systems are intelligent data bases which do not merely regurgitate information, but analyse it. Expert systems are able to provide professional advice to doctors, solicitors, accountants, etc.

Files: A list of relevant information in a computer program or data base.

Formal Operational: A stage in student learning/development where it is possible to understand and work within the abstract.

Graphics: Pictures or diagrams which are shown on the computer screen as opposed to words.

Graphics Tablet: A flat device (tablet) which is connected to the computer screen enabling the user (with the aid of a special pen) to write, draw, paint, teach, or demonstrate via the VDU.

THE THREE Cs

Group Dynamics: The totality of individual interactions determining the behaviour of a group.

Hard Copy: Information from the computer which has been printed out for records or display, etc.

Hardware: The physical devices which comprise the computer and peripherals. Contrast with software.

Holographic: Of three-dimensional images displayed on a picture or screen.

Incompatibility: Computer programs not being transferable from one make of computer to another.

Input: Instructions and data entered (put into) a computer.

Integrated Circuits: An electronic circuit which is manufactured as a whole (integrated) unit, rather than made up of separate parts (e.g. transistors, capacitors, resistors, etc.) which are subsequently wired up together. Integrated circuits can be miniaturized as when they are etched onto a silicon chip.

Intelligent Data bases: Interactive data bases which may reorganize the information stored. They are intermediate between ordinary data bases and expert systems.

Interactive: Of a dialogue between the user and the computer or other device.

Interface: A device or system at which other devices or systems interact. For example, a modem may represent the interface between a computer and a telephone.

Joystick: A lever which may be moved so as to allow the user to move the cursor on the screen, bypassing the conventional keyboard.

Light Pen: A pen which allows the user to write directly on a computer's screen.

Liveware: People who work or interact with computers such as computer salesmen, teachers, pupils, etc.

LOGO: A programming language especially designed for children. It is particularly used as a means of controlling Turtles, but may be used for other kinds of programs as well.

Memory: The storage capacity of a computer, tape or disk, usually expressed in terms of kilobytes (thousands of bytes), or megabytes (millions of bytes).

Microwriter: A word processor with only six keys and a very small display area. It can be plugged into a larger VDU and several can be used by a group of children to interact with each other via the computer.

Modem: A device to connect hardware together, usually computers to telephones.

Output: Answers, data, graphics, electronic pulses, etc. emanating from a computer.

Output Device: May include a TV screen, loudspeaker, tape recorder, printer, robot, simple switch, etc.

Peer Teaching: When children of the same age teach or help each other with a particular piece of work or computer program.

Peripherals: Used to describe all attachments to the computer, e.g., printer, disk, audio cassette, joystick, lightpen, modem, etc.

208

Program: Precise logical instructions which enables the computer to perform a particular function or task. Initially, the instructions are placed in the computer, but can then be saved either on tape or disk, or printed out as hard copy.

Qwerty keyboard: Standard typewriter keyboard, so named because the top left-hand letters spell out QWERTY.

Readability: A measure enabling teachers/parents to find out whether a book is at the appropriate level of understanding for the children in their care.

Real Time: Pertains to the virtually instantaneous response of computers and the transmission of electronic data, at the speed of light.

Retrieval Systems: Systems for recovering (retrieving) stored information from a receptacle. Such a receptacle of information can be other people, books, filing cabinets, computers, data bases, etc.

Robot: A mechanical device activated and controlled by computers. It can either be attached to the computer or be remote-controlled.

Simulation: Data and graphics presented on the computer to reflect 'real-life' situations, which enable the user to react and work out solutions to the given situation, e.g. flight simulations, patient symptoms, etc.

Software: Programs and data used to control computers. Computer software is to hardware what the music on a tape is to the tape player.

Teaching Machines: A device providing programmed instruction. Usually associated with drill and practice.

Terminal: An individual computer from which, and to which, information is passed as part of a computer network.

Turtle: A robot which can be controlled by computer. The language used to control the robot is LOGO. There is also a tiny screen image called 'turtle' which is moved around on the screen and may act as the interface for graphics.

VDU (Visual Display Unit): A screen, either a monitor or television set which displays information relayed from the computer as words or graphics. Same as the American CRT.

Useful Addresses (for British readers)

1. Computers in Education, Group of Artificial Intelligence
   University of Edinburgh
   SCOTLAND
2. Computers in Education as a Resource (CEDAR)
   Imperial College Computer Centre
   Exhibition Road
   LONDON SW7 2BX
3. Council of Education Technology (CET)
   3 Devonshire Road
   LONDON W1N 2BA
4. Gifted Children's Information Centre
   941 Warwick Road
   SOLIHULL
   West Midlands B91 3EX
5. Institute for Educational Technology
   The Open University,
   Walton Hall
   MILTON KEYNES
   Bucks MK7 6AA
6. Maths Education Centre
   Upper Bognor Road
   BOGNOR, Sussex
7. Microelectronics Education Programme (MEP)
   Cheviot House
   Coach Lane Campus
   NEWCASTLE UPON TYNE NE7 7XA
8. National Association for the Teaching of English (NATE)
   49 Broomgrove Road
   SHEFFIELD S10 2NA
9. *SEMERCS*
   (a) Newcastle SEMERC, Newcastle Polytechnic, Coach Lane Campus, NEWCASTLE UPON TYNE NE7 7XA
   (b) Manchester SEMERC, Manchester Polytechnic, Hathersage Road, MANCHESTER M13 0JA

(c) Bristol SEMERC, Faculty of Education, Bristol Polytechnic, Redland Hill, BRISTOL BS6 6UZ
(d) Redbridge SEMERC, Dane Centre, c/o The Teachers' Centre, Melbourne Road, ILFORD, Essex G1 4HJ

Some British Software Houses

Acornsoft Ltd, 4a Market Hill, CAMBRIDGE BC2 3JN

Addison Wesley, 53 Bedford Square, LONDON WC1B 3DZ

Advisory Unit for Computer-based Education (AUCBE), Endymion Road, HATFIELD, Herts

Applied Systems Knowledge (ASK) London House, 68 Upper Richmond Road, LONDON SW15 2RP

Aztec, 25 St Mark's Road, Deepcar, SHEFFIELD

BBC Software, 35 Marylebone High Street, LONDON W1M 4AA

Bourne Educational Software, Bourne House, The Hundred, Romsey, Hamps. SO5 8BY

Cambridge University Press, The Edinburgh Building, Shaftesbury Avenue, CAMBRIDGE CB2 2LY

Chalksoft, Lowmoor Cottage, Tonedale, WELLINGTON, Somerset TA21 0AL

Computer Concepts, 16 Wayside, CHIPPERFIELD, Herts WD4 9JJ

Corona Software, 73 High Road, South Woodford, LONDON E18 2AP

ESM Software, Duke Street, Wisbech, CAMBRIDGE PE13 2AE

4MATION Educational Resources, Lindea Lea, Rock Park, BARNSTAPLE, Devon EX32 9AQ

Garland Computing, 35 Dean Hill, PLYMOUTH PL9 9AF

Ginn Microcomputer Software, Prebendal House, Parson's Fee, AYLESBURY, Bucks HP20 2QZ

Heinemann Computers in Education, 22 Bedford Square, LONDON WC1B 3HH

John Wiley Software, Baffins Lane, CHICHESTER, Sussex PO19 1VD

Kansas City Systems, Unit 3, Sutton Springs Wood, CHESTERFIELD, S44 5XF

Ladybird Longman MicroSoftware, Longman Group Resource Unit, 33–35 Tanner Row, YORK YO1 1JP

Some British Software Houses

Newman College Primary Software, c/o Roger Keeling, Newman College, Bartley Green, BIRMINGHAM B32 3NT

Specialised Education & Software Services, 18 Luccombe Hill, Redland, BRISTOL BS9 3JE

Tecmedia Ltd, 5 Granby Street, LOUGHBOROUGH, Leicestershire LE11 3DW

Valiant Designs Ltd, Park House, 140 Battersea Park Road, LONDON SW11 4NB

Index

214